BLACKBIRD

BAKERY GLUTEN-FREE

BLACKBIRD BAKERY GLUTEN-FREE

75 Recipes for Irresistible Desserts and Pastries

By KAREN MORGAN

Photographs by Knoxy

CHRONICLE BOOKS

SAN FRANCISCO

Text copyright © 2010 by Karen Morgan.
Photographs copyright © 2010 by Knox Photographics.

Library of Congress Cataloging-in-Publication Data available.
ISBN 978-0-8118-7331-4

Manufactured in China

Designed by Blair Richardson, Little Mule Studio
The photographer wishes to thank: My God—my soul and my strength; my incredible
family, who has given me such steadfast support: my mum, Joy, and my pops, Randy;
Esther and Raychel for your rockstar assistance; Phyllis for breathing life into our
August shoot; Justin Vernon, whose music provided the soundtrack to this period of
my life and work; and Karen—truly one of the kindest people I have had the pleasure
of knowing and working with.

10 9 8 7 6 5 4 3 2

Chronicle Books LLC
680 Second Street
San Francisco, California 94107
www.chroniclebooks.com

GLYCERIN

An elegant application for chapped hands,
face and lips.

MORGAN'S PHARMACY
Rexall
TECUMSEH,   OKLA.

dedication

I would like to dedicate this work to my son, Leo, the bright
light that led me back to the lee shore.

In memory of my beloved nephew and friend, Andy Morgan,
who left us too soon.

"Remember, once is forever."
—Andrew Morgan (July 25, 1979 to June 22, 2005)

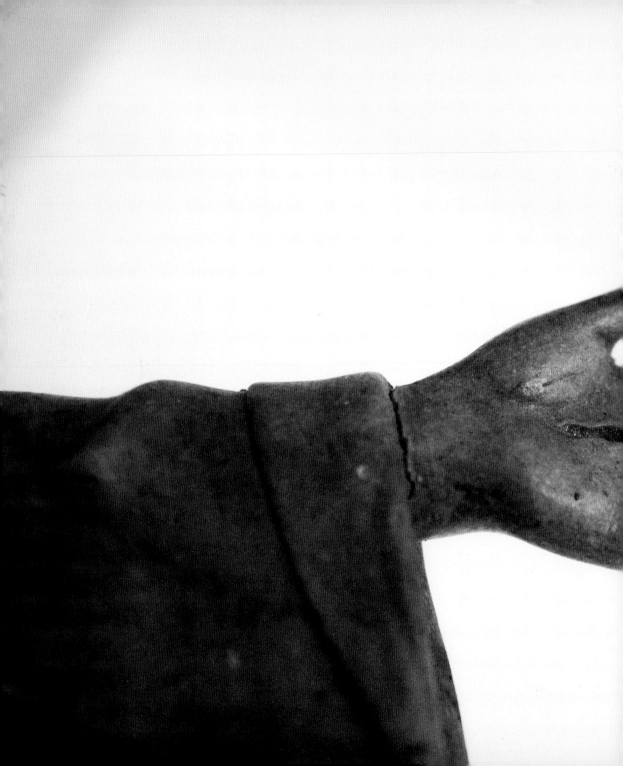

acknowledgments

First and foremost, I would like to thank my mother and my grandmother for filling me with the passion to cook and the magic to make it happen.

I would also like to thank Tim Morgan and the entire Morgan family for their patient palates over the years as my recipes came to life.

In truth, this book would not be a reality without the love and support that I have received from the following people: Lisa Hickey, for giving me that first chance and her years of unwavering support; Dave Marglin, for his guidance, patience, and profound intellect; David and Cindy Price, for that life-changing summer cooking for them in France; Allison Walsh, for reminding me that less is definitely more; my parents, for bringing me into the world; my brothers and sisters, for keeping me company along the way; my editors at Chronicle Books, Bill LeBlond and Sarah Billingsley, for seeing my potential and helping me actualize it; Marcy Posner at Sterling Lord Literistic, for the very same reason; Knoxy, for her vision and photographic brilliance; Joy, for giving birth to Knoxy; Phyllis, for her creative input; Blair Richardson, for her beautiful graphic design work; Hunter Cross, for my Web support; Liz Lambert of the Hotel St. Cecilia, for allowing us to photograph there; Barry of Howl, for his generous spirit; Steve and the crew from Uncommon Objects, for having such fabulous taste; Merritt Loughran Meade, for helping catapult Blackbird Bakery into the consciousness of people; and every single other person I have encountered in the last seven years, as it is from these relationships that I found my true calling.

contents

introduction

MY AIM FOR THIS BOOK IS VERY SIMPLE: to provide hope for those who, like myself, suffer from autoimmune disorders like celiac disease, or any other medical condition—such as autism, Asperger's syndrome, ADD, and ADHD—that may require a change of diet. The latest research reveals that a growing number of cancer treatments are significantly more effective when the patients are placed on a gluten-free diet.

So how does one make such a radical change in their diet and still find pleasure in food? The act of eating is one of the highest forms of pleasure in the tableaux of human experience. When this aspect of my life was taken from me, I immediately took note. The seemingly simple act of eating became a complex, frustrating task, rather than a moment of pleasure. I set out to reclaim this birthright, and here, in these pages, you will find that life without gluten can be just as good, if not better, than what came before.

At the time of my diagnosis in 2002, the available gluten-free products were so unsatisfactory, I took it upon myself to do something about it. After seven years of loving experimentation and exhaustive research, including living and working in France, launching a food blog, and opening my online bakeshop, Blackbird Bakery, I have compiled this compendium of recipes that are so delicious you will forget that you are eating gluten-free.

Most important, I wanted to find a way to take away that helpless feeling from those who are newly diagnosed, empowering all of us with the knowledge that life is still full of edible pleasure. May this be your road map!

Life is mutable, but our greatest strength lies in our ability to adapt to these changes in an intelligent way. It is my hope that you will find *Blackbird Bakery Gluten-Free* to be part of the solution to this ever-growing problem.

AT LAST! ENJOY!

BAKING GLUTEN-FREE

In traditional baking, gluten—the protein found in wheat flour—expands and contracts in a series of chemical reactions. These reactions produce the springy texture that creates light, moist breads, rolls, and cakes. So what is one to do when this elastic protein is not present in flour?

Take heart, for gluten-free baking is possible. This book uses the following basic techniques for making your own delicious gluten-free baked goods:

First and foremost, as many whole-grain flours as possible are used in each recipe; these work together to provide both structure and good nutrition. Guar gum is used in combination with the flours to give elasticity to the doughs and batters; this provides the necessary structure to leaven the baked goods.

I am a huge believer in using only organic products. I use only organic produce, dairy products (including eggs), and flours when possible in my everyday life and for my customers. Organic foods have the nutrients we need for overall health (minus the additives that can negatively affect our health), and what's more, they taste better. And as a baker and chef, if it doesn't taste good, then I don't want it.

notes on ingredients

Here is a list of the gluten-free flours used in this book, along with other special ingredients found in the recipes.

ALMOND FLOUR/MEAL

Almond flour is usually made from blanched almonds, while almond meal may be made from either blanched or raw almonds; the two are interchangeable. Almond flour/meal provides excellent flavor and creates a moist crumb.

AMARANTH FLOUR

Whole-grain amaranth was a staple for the Incas and Aztecs. Like buckwheat and quinoa, amaranth is a complete protein containing a complete set of amino acids. It has 30 percent more protein than rice, wheat flour, oats, or rye. Use sparingly; its flavor is distinctively earthy, and its texture is quite granular.

CHESTNUT FLOUR

Made from ground chestnuts, this flour is low in fat and high in fiber. It has a strong nutty flavor, so you may want to use it sparingly, but I love it.

GARBANZO BEAN FLOUR

Made from ground chickpeas (also known as garbanzo beans) one of the oldest cultivated vegetables, dating back seventy-five hundred years. Indian cuisine relies heavily on this flour for its various flat breads, and the Italians use it to make a flat bread known as *socca*. It has an intense earthy odor, which can be hard to conceal in sweet baked goods; however, it works wonderfully in conjunction with pureed fruits in gluten-free breads and muffins.

GLUTINOUS RICE FLOUR

A flour made from ground sticky rice, sweet rice, waxy rice, botan rice, biroin chal, mochi rice, and/or pearl rice. These rice varieties, cultivated in Japan, Korea, China, the Philippines, Thailand, Laos, Indonesia, and Vietnam, date back eleven thousand years. Glutinous rice flour is easily attainable at most Asian markets and is very inexpensive. It is virtually odorless, and is an excellent way to attain a light, moist texture in gluten-free baked goods.

MILLET FLOUR

First cultivated in East Asia over ten thousand years ago, millet is one of the oldest grains in the human diet. Rich in B vitamins, especially niacin, B_6, and folic acid, along with calcium, iron, potassium, magnesium, and zinc, it is exceptionally nutritious. Today, millet is widely used in western India to make flat breads, and in China and Russia for porridge. Pale yellow in color, millet flour is mild in flavor and produces excellent texture in baked goods.

SORGHUM FLOUR

Native to Ethiopia and Sudan, sorghum was brought to the United States as "guinea corn" from West Africa by slave traders around 1850. Prized for its high protein and fiber content, it also has a low level of carbohydrates, making it a wonderful source of energy. This flour has a nutty, subtly sweet flavor, and adds depth to any baked treat. It is sometimes marketed as "sweet white" sorghum flour.

TAPIOCA FLOUR

Derived from the yucca or cassava root, tapioca flour is typically used as a thickening agent and has the color and texture of fine talcum powder. Used extensively throughout Brazil and South America, it is also used throughout this book. The flavor is mild, but becomes very strong when used in conjunction with chocolate.

CLARIFIED BUTTER

The clear butterfat from melted butter, used when you want to heat butter to a high heat without browning it. To make clarified butter: In a small, heavy saucepan, melt 1 cup (2 sticks) unsalted butter over low heat. Remove from the heat and skim the foam from the top. Pour the clear yellow liquid (the butterfat) into a glass jar, leaving the milky layer in the bottom (the milk fat). Cover and refrigerate indefinitely. Makes ⅔ cup.

CORNSTARCH

The starch derived from corn. Prized for its thickening properties, it is widely used in gravies and other sauces. In gluten-free cooking, cornstarch aids in thickening batters and dough. For those who suffer from corn allergies, arrowroot can be substituted in equal parts.

CULTURED BUTTER

Butter made from fermented butterfat. During fermentation, the cream naturally sours as bacteria convert milk sugars to lactic acid, resulting in a much rounder, fuller butter flavor.

GLUTEN-FREE OATS

Oats that are grown on gluten-free dedicated farms and planted with non-GMO seed stock. Buy only oats labeled "gluten-free," as other oats may have been processed or stored in containers that have held wheat flour. Finely ground, gluten-free oats make a great flour.

GUAR GUM

Made from the ground seeds of the guar bean. A water-soluble fiber, guar gum is recommended for overall intestinal health. It has very little odor, making it a great addition to baked goods. More importantly, guar gum is an excellent stabilizer, providing elasticity and structure to gluten-free baked goods. I prefer it to pungent-smelling xanthum gum, which is used as a stabilizer in many gluten-free products.

MEXICAN VANILLA

Vanilla beans from Mexico are especially strong in flavor, both in the bean and in vanilla extract.

ORGANIC BUTTERMILK

Buttermilk adds tenderness and moisture to baked goods, but only organic buttermilk is gluten-free. Nonorganic buttermilk contains modified food starch, a gluten-based ingredient.

SANDING SUGAR

A coarse-grained sugar used for decorative purposes.

TEXAS PECANS

These nuts are far sweeter in flavor than pecans from neighboring Southern states, where their notes tend to be more bitter.

VIETNAMESE CINNAMON

Vietnamese cinnamon has a much higher oil content than other varieties, resulting in a more pronounced flavor that pervades rather than fades.

XYLITOL

Birch sugar can be substituted in the cookie and cake recipes for those on a low-glycemic diet. I don't recommend substituting in the custards and puddings.

CHAPTER ONE

biscuits, muffins & sweet breads

popovers

These popovers are absolutely to die for. Their respectably crisp exterior gives way to a helplessly fluffy center where the custard flavor of the eggs really shines through. The popovers are appropriate anytime, whether slathered with fresh preserves and butter for breakfast or eaten plain with dinner. Either way, you and your guests will be flabbergasted that they are gluten-free!

MAKES 12 POPOVERS

Note: Use clarified butter to prepare the pan, as regular butter can burn and smoke at the high temperature used for these popovers.

Position an oven rack in the center of the oven. Preheat the oven to 425°F. Grease the popover cups with vegetable shortening. Spoon a little of the clarified butter into each of 12 popover or muffin cups, just enough to cover the bottom of each cup.

In a large bowl, combine all the dry ingredients and stir with a whisk to combine. In a separate bowl, whisk together the eggs and the milk. Pour the egg mixture over the dry ingredients and briskly whisk until smooth. Add the melted butter and whisk just until incorporated.

Fill the prepared popover cups about two-thirds full with the batter and bake for 15 minutes. Reduce the oven temperature to 325°F and continue baking for an additional 5 minutes, or until the tops of the popovers have risen over the tops of the pan and are golden brown.

Remove from the oven and unmold the popovers onto a wire rack to cool. Serve warm or at room temperature.

Make the day of serving and store by wrapping them in a cloth.

INGREDIENTS

solid vegetable shortening

¼ cup clarified unsalted butter (page 15)

1 cup millet flour

1 cup glutinous rice flour

1 teaspoon guar gum

1 teaspoon baking powder

1 teaspoon kosher salt

2 tablespoons confectioners' sugar

6 large eggs, beaten

2 cups whole milk

2 tablespoons unsalted butter, melted

sunday morning pancakes

My search for the perfect Sunday morning pancakes has been a lesson in patience more than anything. I have to say that the waiting has paid off tremendously, as these babies are the ideal version of the weekend morning staple! They rise up and hold their height with a soft, fluffy texture. Their flavor is so phenomenal, you'll glow with pride when you see that every last one has been devoured by your hungry guests.

MAKES 8 BIG PANCAKES OR 16 SMALL ONES

In a large bowl, combine all the dry ingredients and stir with a whisk to blend. Add the eggs, buttermilk, and melted butter and stir until smooth.

Heat a large skillet or a griddle over medium-low heat. Spray the pan with safflower oil spray. Run your hands under the faucet to wet your fingertips and then shake them over the hot griddle. If the water dances across the pan, the heat is just right to begin making your pancakes. For each large pancake, pour ¼ cup batter into the pan; for small pancakes, use 2 tablespoons batter. Cook until bubbles form on the top of each pancake; turn and cook until golden brown on the bottom. Transfer to a baking sheet and keep warm in a 200°F oven while cooking the remaining batter.

To save time , mix all the dry ingredients in advance and keep in an airtight container in a cool dry place for up to 3 months.

BLACKBIRD BAKING TIP

This versatile recipe can be customized into whatever type of pancake you are craving. Try adding fresh fruit, such as ½ cup of blueberries or bananas, and a few dashes of cinnamon or ½ cup chocolate chips. Add ground spice directly to the batter and whisk to incorporate. When adding fresh fruit or chocolate, simply sprinkle some on top of each pancake before you flip it. After your first batch, you'll find yourself thinking, "Gluten? Who needs it?"

INGREDIENTS

- ¼ cup plus 2 tablespoons almond flour
- ½ cup millet flour
- 2 tablespoons glutinous rice flour
- 2 tablespoons sugar
- 1 teaspoon guar gum
- ½ teaspoon kosher salt
- ½ teaspoon baking soda
- ½ teaspoon baking powder
- 2 large eggs, beaten
- 1 cup organic buttermilk
- 2 tablespoons unsalted butter, melted

safflower oil cooking spray

1 teaspoon unflavored gelatin

1½ cups organic buttermilk

1 cup sorghum flour

1 cup cornstarch

½ cup tapioca flour

¼ cup glutinous rice flour,
   plus more for dusting

2 teaspoons baking powder

½ teaspoon baking soda

2 teaspoons guar gum

½ teaspoon plus ⅛ teaspoon
   kosher salt

⅓ cup granulated sugar

½ cup (1 stick) cold unsalted
   butter, diced, plus
   2 tablespoons, melted

grated zest of 1 lemon

4 slices dried pears, diced

1 cup dried cranberries

sanding sugar for sprinkling

cranberry-pear scones

My mom was an avid consumer of scones until we were both diagnosed with celiac disease. Then, like a plethora of other beloved foods, scones disappeared, literally overnight, from our repertoire. After years of torture (walking past bakeries and not being able to buy a single thing, let alone our beloved scones!), I devised this recipe, and the word *scone* was allowed, at long last, to be uttered in our presence. Wanting to really knock my mom's socks off, I filled them with some of her favorite dried fruit—pears and cranberries—for an alternative to the customary currants.

MAKES 9 SCONES

Position an oven rack in the center of the oven. Preheat the oven to 400°F. Liberally butter a baking sheet.

In a measuring cup, sprinkle the gelatin over the buttermilk and allow to soften for at least 10 minutes. Using a small whisk, stir the gelatin into the buttermilk to prevent any clumping.

In a large bowl, combine all the dry ingredients and stir with a whisk to blend. Add the ½ cup butter and, using a pastry cutter, cut into the dry ingredients until the butter resembles small peas. Add the lemon zest, pears, and cranberries. Pour the gelatin mixture over the dry ingredients and stir until the dough is a sticky, tacky ball.

Dust a work surface with glutinous rice flour and turn the dough out onto it. Dust the top of the dough with glutinous rice flour and knead the dough about 3 turns, or until it is no longer sticky.

Shape the dough into a rectangle 12 inches long and 5 inches wide. Brush with the melted butter and then sprinkle with the sanding sugar. Cut the rectangle into 9 triangles and then transfer the scones to the prepared pan. You can cut the dough into rounds.

Bake for 20 minutes, or until lightly golden, rotating the pan after 15 minutes of baking. Remove from the oven and transfer the scones to wire racks. Serve warm.

These scones can be made a few hours ahead and reheated in a low oven.

BLACKBIRD BAKING TIP

The type of flour used for rolling out dough for gluten-free baking is extremely important. I always use either glutinous rice flour or tapioca flour. I recommend avoiding cornstarch, as it has a tendency to create a rubbery coating that is highly unpalatable and can ruin all your hard work.

buttermilk biscuits

When I was a little girl, making biscuits was one of my favorite things to do because they were so easy and so delicious. Not until I began my experiments with gluten-free baking did I realize the gift my mother and grandmother had passed on to me in the process: They taught me that in making the very best biscuits, it was all about the touch. The less you touched the dough, the better the biscuits. If you over-kneaded the dough, the biscuits would be much drier and would turn to stone twice as fast. So as you are kneading your dough, remember less is more, and you will have those moist, mouthwatering biscuits you've been dreaming about.

Any of the suggested accompaniments you choose will sing atop this Southern classic.

MAKES ABOUT 8 LARGE BISCUITS

Position an oven rack in the center of the oven. Preheat the oven to 425°F. In a large bowl, combine all the dry ingredients and stir with a whisk to blend. Add the butter and vegetable shortening. Using a pastry cutter, cut the fats into your dry ingredients until the mixture resembles small peas.

Stir in the buttermilk until the dough forms a ball. If the mixture is too dry, stir in the water 1 tablespoon at a time. Turn your dough out onto a work surface dusted with tapioca flour and knead until very smooth, 3 to 4 turns. Form the dough into a disk 1 inch thick. Using a 3-inch-diameter biscuit cutter, cut out biscuits and arrange them in an unbuttered 9-inch cake pan. Bake for 12 to 15 minutes, or until lightly golden brown. Remove from the oven and transfer the biscuits to wire racks to cool briefly.

Serve hot, with butter, agave syrup, or preserves of your choice.

To store: Place in a storage container with a lid. Store in a cool, dry place for up to 2 days.

INGREDIENTS

½ cup sorghum flour

1 cup cornstarch

½ cup tapioca flour, plus ¼ cup for dusting

1 teaspoon guar gum

½ teaspoon kosher salt

1 tablespoon baking powder

3 tablespoons cold unsalted butter, diced

3 tablespoons cold vegetable shortening, preferably non-hydrogenated, diced

1 cup organic buttermilk

2 to 3 tablespoons water, if needed

salted butter, agave syrup, or fruit preserves for serving

apple-pumpkin muffins

INGREDIENTS

- 1 cup sorghum flour
- ½ cup cornstarch
- ½ cup tapioca flour
- 2 teaspoons guar gum
- 2 teaspoons baking powder
- ¼ teaspoon kosher salt
- 1 cup granulated sugar
- 1 tablespoon dark brown sugar
- ½ cup packed light brown sugar
- 2⅛ teaspoons ground cinnamon
- ½ teaspoon freshly grated nutmeg
- 1½ teaspoons ground ginger
- ¾ cup (1½ sticks) unsalted butter at room temperature
- 2 large eggs, beaten
- one 15-ounce can solid-pack unsweetened pumpkin
- 1 tablespoon pure vanilla extract
- 1 Golden Delicious apple, peeled, cored, and finely diced

My favorite time of year to enjoy muffins is in the early fall, when the cooler winds start picking up and the smell of wood smoke marks the first log fires of the season. That's when I like to head indoors, make these wholly satisfying muffins, brew some good strong cider or coffee, and build a fire of my own.

MAKES 18 TO 24 MUFFINS

Position an oven rack in the center of the oven. Preheat the oven to 350°F. Line muffin cups with paper liners.

In a medium bowl, combine all the dry ingredients, including the sugars and spices, and stir with a whisk to blend.

In a stand mixer fitted with the paddle attachment, cream the butter on medium-high speed until soft. Add the dry ingredients all at once and mix on low speed for about 2 minutes. Add the eggs, pumpkin, and vanilla and mix on medium-high speed until light and fluffy, stopping to scrape down the sides of the bowl several times. Stir in the apple. Using an ice-cream scoop, fill the prepared muffin cups three-fourths full with batter and bake for 25 minutes, or until cracked on top and browned on the edges. A wooden skewer inserted into one of the muffins will come out clean.

BLACKBIRD BAKING TIP

I recommend using organic canned pumpkin. It is less watery than the non-organic variety.

To store: Place in a sealable container and refrigerate for up to 3 days.

cottage cheese muffins with hickory-smoked bacon and chives

These muffins were inspired by my exercise buddy, Amy, who was searching high and low for a particular cottage cheese muffin she had tried while traveling. She wanted a muffin that was light and fluffy, with the cottage cheese not only visible but present in flavor as well. After five batches, I came up with a working recipe, which was delicious, but still missing something. Once bacon and chives entered the equation, I had found the point of no return. Whenever people try these, their first and only response is "Oh my god, what are these?" These are best the day they are baked.

MAKES 12 MUFFINS

Position an oven rack in the center of the oven. Preheat the oven to 375°F. Line 12 muffin cups with paper liners.

In a medium skillet, fry the bacon over medium heat until crisp. Using a slotted spoon, transfer the bacon to paper towels to drain.

In a stand mixer fitted with the paddle attachment, combine all the dry ingredients and mix on low speed. Add the butter and continue to mix for 2 minutes, or until blended.

Add the eggs and vanilla and mix on medium speed until the batter is light and fluffy. Add the milk and mix on high speed until smooth, about 30 seconds. Remove the bowl from the mixer and fold in the cottage cheese, scraping down the sides of the bowl with each fold. Fold in the raisins, chives, and bacon.

Using an ice-cream scoop, fill the prepared muffin cups three-fourths full with batter and bake for 25 minutes, or until the muffins are golden brown and firm to the touch.

Remove from the oven and transfer to a wire rack to cool slightly or completely. Serve warm or at room temperature.

To store: Place in a sealable container and refrigerate for up to 3 days.

INGREDIENTS

- ½ cup finely chopped hickory-smoked bacon (about 4 slices)
- ¼ cup sorghum flour
- ¼ cup almond meal
- ½ cup cornstarch
- 1 cup tapioca flour
- ½ cup packed light brown sugar
- ¼ cup granulated sugar
- ¼ teaspoon kosher salt
- 2 teaspoons guar gum
- 2 teaspoons baking powder
- ½ cup (1 stick) unsalted butter at room temperature
- 2 large eggs
- 1 teaspoon pure vanilla extract
- ½ cup whole milk
- 1½ cups low-fat cottage cheese
- 1 cup raisins
- ¼ cup minced fresh chives

southern-style corn bread

The mere idea of going through the holidays without a stuffing for the bird was such an impossibility that I promptly set out to fill the void with a gluten-free one. I decided to go the corn bread route, as I wanted to create a corn bread that was delicious all on its own, while having the capacity to become the star in a holiday stuffing. Not only is this corn bread easy to make, it's just flat-out delicious. You'll fall in love after the first bite, filled as it is with flecks of golden sweetness thanks to the whole-kernel corn and a moist, tangy crumb thanks to the buttermilk.

MAKES ONE 8-BY-8-INCH LOAF

Position an oven rack in the center of the oven. Preheat the oven to 425°F. Liberally grease an 8-inch square baking pan with bacon fat. Set aside.

In a large bowl, combine all the dry ingredients and stir with a whisk to blend. Stir in the eggs, buttermilk, and butter. Mix until smooth. Fold in the corn kernels. Pour into the prepared pan, loosely cover with aluminum foil, and bake for 25 to 30 minutes, or until a wooden skewer inserted into the center comes out clean. Remove from the oven, let cool slightly, and cut into squares. Serve warm or at room temperature.

BLACKBIRD BAKING TIP

To use for a corn bread dressing or stuffing, crumble the corn bread and spread it out on a baking sheet. Cover with a kitchen towel and let dry overnight.

corn bread muffins

MAKES 12 MUFFINS

Grease 12 muffin cups with either bacon fat or butter or line them with paper liners. Fill the prepared cups three-fourths full with the batter and bake in a preheated 425°F oven for 15 to 20 minutes, or until lightly golden brown.

INGREDIENTS

bacon fat for greasing pan

1¼ cups stone-ground cornmeal

½ cup sorghum flour

½ cup cornstarch

⅓ cup glutinous rice flour

2 teaspoons guar gum

2½ teaspoons baking powder

1 teaspoon kosher salt

¼ cup sugar

2 large eggs, beaten

1½ cups organic buttermilk

4 tablespoons unsalted butter, melted

one 15-ounce can whole-kernel corn, drained, or 2 cups fresh or thawed frozen corn kernels

texas pecan–banana bread

INGREDIENTS

4 very ripe bananas

1½ cups Bob's Red Mill all-
    purpose gluten-free flour

1 cup sugar

1 teaspoon baking soda

1 teaspoon kosher salt

½ cup (1 stick) unsalted butter
    at room temperature

2 large eggs

⅔ cup organic buttermilk

2 teaspoons pure vanilla
    extract

⅔ cup chopped pecans,
    preferably from Texas

Cream Cheese Icing (page 38;
    optional)

My banana bread recipe is important to me for many reasons, but the primary source of my pride resides in the simple fact that this was the recipe that compelled me to become a gluten-free baker. It sounds silly in retrospect, but in truth, after I found success in creating something so delicious when everything that came before fell short, I felt hope rise up within me that maybe, just maybe, life was going to be beautiful once again.

This bread is divine right out of the oven with melted butter, supreme when toasted with a little butter and honey, and sinful with cream cheese icing.

MAKES ONE 5-BY-9 INCH LOAF

Position an oven rack in the center of the oven. Preheat the oven to 350°F. Line a rimmed baking sheet with aluminum foil. Butter a 5-by-9-inch loaf pan.

Arrange the bananas in a row on the prepared baking sheet. Using a paring knife, pierce the top of each banana six times. Roast for 15 minutes, or until the skin of the bananas is black and bulging, with juices oozing from the vents you created prior to roasting.

Remove from the oven and let the bananas cool completely on the pan. To remove the insides, have a medium bowl ready. Take one of the roasted bananas, hold it over the bowl and begin peeling the roasted skin. The flesh of the banana should fall out seamlessly. Run your fingers along the interior of the skins, as you would a squeegee down a windowpane, to extract the caramelized juices. Mash the bananas with a fork or a potato masher until no large clumps are visible. Set aside.

In a stand mixer fitted with the paddle attachment, combine the flour, sugar, baking soda, and salt and mix on low speed to blend. Add the butter and continue to mix on low speed until blended. Add the eggs and mix on medium speed until smooth. Reduce the speed to low, immediately add the buttermilk, and gradually bring the mixer up to high speed until the batter is light and fluffy, stopping once or twice to scrape down the sides of the bowl. Add the banana pulp, vanilla, and pecans. Stir to blend. Pour into the prepared loaf pan and loosely cover with aluminum foil. Bake for 1 hour 15 minutes, or until a wooden skewer inserted in the center of the loaf comes out clean. Remove from the oven. Let cool in the pan for 10 minutes. Run a knife around the sides of the pan and unmold the loaf onto a wire rack and let cool for at least 15 minutes before slicing if serving warm; allow to cool completely if icing.

To store, wrap in aluminum foil or plastic wrap and refrigerate for up to 5 days.

ginger gingerbread

This gingerbread is a gorgeous way to warm even the coldest of hearts, as it is brimming with spices that are aromatic and satisfying. The flavor is layered and complex, with ginger in two different forms, making it all the more indulgent. One bite is never enough, very much like love.

MAKES ONE 5-BY-9-INCH LOAF

Position an oven rack in the center of the oven. Preheat the oven to 350°F. Liberally butter a 5-by-9-inch loaf pan.

In a stand mixer fitted with the paddle attachment, combine all the dry ingredients, including the sugars and spices, and mix on low speed to blend evenly. Add the butter and mix until blended. Add the fresh ginger, buttermilk, molasses, eggs, and vanilla and mix on medium-high speed until light and fluffy. Fold in the crystallized ginger.

Transfer the batter to the prepared pan, smooth the top, and cover loosely with aluminum foil. Bake for 45 minutes, or until browned and a wooden skewer inserted into the center of the bread comes out clean.

Remove from the oven and let cool in the pan for 10 minutes. Unmold onto a wire rack and let cool slightly or completely. Cut into slices and serve warm or at room temperature.

BLACKBIRD BAKING TIP

You can also bake this in an 8-by-8-inch square pan. Simply reduce the baking time to 25 to 30 minutes.

lemon-infused pound cake

Oh, the pound cake—at once so familiar yet so confoundedly elusive in the world of gluten-free baking. I've never seen it in any gluten-free bakeries or in any gluten-free freezer sections at the grocery store. It took me four days, seven attempts, and $65 worth of butter before I could consider my creation a success. I kept my approach very basic. Serve with fresh berries and Chantilly cream or frost with Cream Cheese Icing (page 38) as a dessert, with acacia honey or strawberry preserves for a breakfast treat.

MAKES ONE 5-BY-9-INCH CAKE

Position an oven rack in the center of the oven. Preheat the oven to 325°F. Butter a 5-by-9-inch loaf pan.

In a medium bowl, combine both flours, the cornstarch, baking powder, and salt and stir with a whisk to blend. Add the lemon zest to the dry ingredients.

In a stand mixer fitted with the paddle attachment, cream the butter and sugar on high speed for 5 minutes. Add the eggs, one at a time, and beat for a full minute after each addition, stopping once or twice to scrape down the sides of the bowl. Reduce the mixer speed to medium and add the dry ingredients all at once; beat for 3 to 5 minutes, or until light and fluffy. Beat in the vanilla. Pour into the prepared pan, smooth the top, and bake for 60 to 75 minutes, or until the cake is lightly golden brown and a wooden skewer inserted in the center comes out clean. Check the cake after the first 25 minutes of baking; if it has begun to darken, loosely cover with aluminum foil and resume baking.

Remove from the oven and let cool completely in the pan on a wire rack. Run a knife around the edges of the pan and unmold the cake on a cutting board. Cut into slices to serve.

BLACKBIRD BAKING TIP

The pound cake was named for the original list of ingredients: a pound of butter, a pound of sugar, and a pound of flour. Obviously you need to use the best. The sugar and flour are no-brainers. But the butter? You want to use a butter that is cultured and has an above-average fat content (84 percent or higher) because it provides additional moisture and a more rounded, buttery flavor. Cultured butters include the French butters Celles sur Belles and Echire, as well as one from the American company Organic Valley.

INGREDIENTS

- 1 cup sorghum flour
- ½ cup tapioca flour
- ½ cup cornstarch
- ½ teaspoon baking powder
- ¼ teaspoon kosher salt
- zest of 1 lemon
- 1 cup (2 sticks) plus 2 tablespoons unsalted cultured butter at room temperature (see Tip)
- 1¼ cups sugar
- 4 large eggs
- 2½ teaspoons pure vanilla extract

cream cheese icing

MAKES ABOUT 2 CUPS

4 tablespoons unsalted butter at room temperature

8 ounces cream cheese at room temperature

1 cup confectioners' sugar, sifted

½ teaspoon pure vanilla extract

In a stand mixer fitted with the paddle attachment, cream the butter on medium-high speed until smooth. Add the cream cheese and continue to mix until smooth. Reduce the speed to low and gradually beat in the sugar until smooth, then add the vanilla and beat on high until light and fluffy.

CHAPTER TWO

cookies & bars

icebox cookies

¾ cup plus 2 tablespoons granulated sugar

1¼ cups glutinous rice flour, plus more for dusting

1¾ cups millet flour

½ teaspoon plus ⅛ teaspoon kosher salt

2 teaspoons guar gum

1 cup (2 sticks) unsalted butter at room temperature

1 teaspoons pure vanilla extract

1 large egg

sanding sugar or colored sprinkles for coating

These old-fashioned cookies are fabulous because they are buttery and extremely simple. You can make them up to three days in advance of your planned event, or just keep a roll of the dough in the freezer for that unexpected get-together. Slice-and-bake cookies have always appealed to me because they make me feel like a schoolgirl again. Remember those high school nights in the kitchen with the log of ready-made chocolate chip cookie dough? Just you and your girlfriends, prank-calling boys, gossiping, and dunking cookies.

MAKES 2½ DOZEN COOKIES

In a stand mixer fitted with the paddle attachment, combine all the dry ingredients and mix on low speed to blend. Add the butter and mix on low speed until blended. Add the vanilla and the egg and mix on medium-high speed until the dough forms a ball. Transfer the dough to a work surface that has been lightly dusted with glutinous rice flour. Knead two times, no more and no less, and shape the dough into a log. Divide in half and shape each section into two logs, each 10 inches long and 1 inch in diameter. Pour the sanding sugar onto a sheet of waxed paper. Roll the logs in the sugar until evenly coated. Wrap the dough in plastic wrap and refrigerate for at least 8 hours or up to 3 days.

Position an oven rack in the center of the oven. Preheat the oven to 375°F. Line two baking sheets with parchment paper or silicone baking mats.

Remove one of the logs from the fridge, unwrap it, and place it on a cutting board. Using a serrated knife, cut the log into slices ½ inch thick. Place the cookies on the baking sheets. Bake one sheet at a time for 12 minutes, or until the edges of the cookies are lightly colored.

Remove from the oven and let cool on the pan for 5 minutes. Transfer the cookies to a wire rack and let cool completely. Repeat to cut and bake the remaining dough.

Store the dough, well wrapped, in the refrigerator for up to 3 days, or freeze for up to 1 month. Store the cookies in an airtight container for up to 1 week.

ABOUT ICEBOX COOKIES

The icebox cookie takes its name from the days when food was stored in large metal or wooden boxes cooled by blocks of ice.

leo's classic sugar cookies

INGREDIENTS

¼ cup sorghum flour

¾ cup glutinous rice flour

¼ cup tapioca flour, plus more
  for dusting

¼ cup cornstarch

1 cup sugar

2 teaspoons unflavored
  gelatin

2 teaspoons guar gum

¼ teaspoon kosher salt

3 tablespoons vegetable
  shortening, preferably
  nonhydrogenated

4 tablespoons unsalted butter
  at room temperature

2 large egg whites

1½ teaspoons pure almond
  extract

½ teaspoon pure vanilla
  extract

Royal Icing (page 48)

Special equipment:

  Ateco plain stainless
  steel tip No. 5

I named these sugar cookies after my son because he's the one who insisted that I make *calaveras mexicanas,* sugar cookies shaped like a skull and bones, for Halloween (they're traditional in these parts for the Mexican Day of the Dead). Well, how can anyone refuse such a request? The beauty of these sugar cookies is that they actually hold their shape throughout the baking process. Some recipes survive through time for a reason: because they are unflinchingly satisfying and unapologetically comforting, and most of all, simply sublime. Will this gluten-free version of the classic join the ranks? Only time will tell . . . but I humbly beseech you to see for yourself.

MAKES 12 LARGE OR 24 MEDIUM COOKIES

In a stand mixer fitted with the paddle attachment, combine all the dry ingredients and mix on low speed to blend.

Add the vegetable shortening and butter and mix on low speed for about 5 minutes, or until blended. Add the egg whites, almond extract, and vanilla and mix on medium-high speed until the dough pulls away from the sides of the bowl and forms a nice ball.

Empty the dough onto a work surface dusted with tapioca flour. If the dough appears sticky, sprinkle the top with some additional tapioca flour, and knead until smooth. Shape the dough into two disks. Wrap in plastic wrap and refrigerate for at least 3 hours or preferably overnight.

Position an oven rack in the center of the oven. Preheat the oven to 325°F. Line two baking sheets with parchment paper or silicone baking mats.

Let one of the disks sit at room temperature for 10 minutes to soften slightly. Lightly dust a work surface with glutinous rice flour and roll out the dough, rotating and turning it to keep it from sticking. Roll out the dough to a thickness of just under ¼ inch; any thinner and the cookies will not hold their shape.

Using cookie cutters, cut out the cookies and transfer them to the prepared pans. Bake one pan at a time for 7 minutes, or until the edges begin to color. Remove from the oven and allow to cool on the pan for 5 minutes before transferring to a wire rack to cool completely.

To ice cookies, paint a thin layer of Royal Icing over each cookie. Allow base icing to harden, about 15 minutes. Using a pastry bag fitted with a No. 5 tip, draw the designs you desire on each cookie.

Cookies can be stored after the icing has set in an airtight container for up to 1 week.

lemon and rosemary buttermilk cookies

One of the things I appreciate most about these cookies is their demeanor; they are not overly showy, but they are beautiful in their simplicity. The same can be said about their composition. The savory rosemary and the bright lemon will light up your taste buds, and the cookie is so light and subtle, you will find yourself wondering how all that flavor got into your mouth in the first place. I like to serve these with tea or have them passed at parties as they are extremely refreshing little palate cleansers.

MAKES ABOUT 2 DOZEN COOKIES

In a stand mixer fitted with the paddle attachment, combine all the dry ingredients. Add the grated zest of 1 lemon and the rosemary and mix on low speed to blend. Add the butter and mix on low speed for about 3 minutes, or until blended. Increase the mixer speed to medium and beat in the egg, then immediately add the buttermilk and beat until light and fluffy, 1 to 2 minutes. The dough will seem thin, but fear not, this is exactly what you want. Cover and refrigerate for 30 minutes.

Position an oven rack in the center of the oven. Preheat the oven to 350°F. Line two baking sheets with parchment paper or silicone baking mats.

Using a 1½-inch-diameter ice cream scoop, place balls of dough 1½ inches apart on the prepared pans. You should have about 24.

Bake one pan at a time for 10 to 12 minutes, or until the cookies are lightly browned on the edges.

Remove from the oven and leave the cookies on the pan for 5 minutes to set, then transfer them to a wire rack to cool completely.

Using a small offset spatula, apply the icing to each cookie in a circle. This icing sets fast, so immediately decorate each cookie with a pinch each of rosemary and lemon zest.

Store in an airtight container in one layer for up to 3 days.

INGREDIENTS

¼ cup millet flour

¼ cup tapioca flour

¼ cup sorghum flour

¼ cup glutinous rice flour

½ cup cornstarch

¼ cup almond meal

¼ teaspoon baking soda

¼ teaspoon kosher salt

1 cup sugar

1 teaspoon guar gum

zest of 1 lemon, plus more for garnish

1 tablespoon minced fresh rosemary, plus more for garnish

7 tablespoons unsalted butter at room temperature

1 large egg

½ cup organic buttermilk

Lemon Icing (page 49)

royal icing

MAKES 1½ CUPS

2 cups confectioners' sugar, sifted

3 tablespoons meringue powder (see Tip)

¼ cup cool water

food coloring(s) of choice

In a stand mixer fitted with the paddle attachment, beat the sugar, meringue powder, and water together on medium speed until smooth and slightly fluffy, about 3 minutes. For a fluffier icing, beat longer. For a thinner icing, add more water, 1 teaspoon at a time, until you have your desired consistency. Stir in food coloring of your choice, one small drop at a time to find your desired color.

BLACKBIRD BAKING TIP

I use meringue powder here instead of raw egg whites to avoid any food-borne pathogens that could cause illness. Meringue powder, or freeze-dried egg whites, helps to make a nice, firm icing. It is widely available in supermarkets and kitchenware stores.

lemon icing

3   tablespoons fresh lemon juice

2   cups confectioners' sugar, sifted

In a medium bowl, whisk the lemon juice into the sugar until smooth. If the icing is too thick, add a few more drops of lemon juice and whisk to incorporate. Repeat until you have the consistency you desire.

chocolate chip cookies

INGREDIENTS

1¼ cups glutinous rice flour

1¼ cups sorghum flour

½ teaspoon baking powder

2½ teaspoons kosher salt

1 teaspoon guar gum

1½ cups packed light brown sugar

¼ cup plus 1 tablespoon granulated sugar

½ cup (1 stick) plus 2 tablespoons unsalted butter at room temperature

3 large eggs

4 teaspoons pure vanilla extract

2 cups milk chocolate chips

1 cup semisweet chocolate chips

Chocolate chip cookies, by far my most beloved, were the most difficult to make gluten-free and still be delicious. In total, I wrestled with the legendary Toll House/Neiman Marcus goodie *eighty-seven times.* After such an epic battle, I feel as though I can rightly say that these cookies are one of my most cherished achievements. The texture is pristine, with an initial crunch that immediately surrenders to a moist center overflowing with complex, gorgeous chocolate flavor. So get those glasses of milk ready, because with these cookies, you can dunk away as you smile in the face of gluten!

MAKES ABOUT 3 DOZEN COOKIES

In a stand mixer fitted with the paddle attachment, combine all the dry ingredients, including the sugars, and mix on low speed to blend. Add the butter and mix on low speed until blended. Add all the eggs at once along with the vanilla and mix on medium-high speed until light and fluffy. Fold in the chocolate chips until evenly dispersed.

Cover and refrigerate for at least 2 hours or up to 2 days.

Position an oven rack in the center of the oven. Preheat the oven to 325°F. Line two baking sheets with parchment paper or silicone baking mats.

Using a 1½-inch-diameter ice-cream scoop, place mounds of dough 1½ inches apart on the prepared pans. Bake one pan at a time for 13 minutes, or until the cookies are lightly browned on the edges, rotating the pan halfway through baking.

Remove from the oven and let cool on the pan for 5 minutes; transfer the cookies to wire racks to cool completely.

These cookies store perfectly in an airtight container for up to 1 week.

BLACKBIRD BAKING TIP

I like a moist chocolate chip cookie, but if you prefer a crunchier version, simply adjust the baking time from 13 to 17 minutes. Keep in mind that these cookies set as they cool, so be careful not to over-bake them.

oatmeal-raisin cookies

As soon as I learned about gluten-free oats, this was the first thing that I wanted to make with them. Even though I have a laundry list of favorite cookies, oatmeal raisin is definitely my "nostalgia" cookie. I love the way the raisins caramelize while baking, and the chewiness of the oats, delivered on a cloud of cinnamon and brown sugar. These always made me happiest when I was low, and I've always been given the highest praise for this recipe, so therein lies the balance, I suppose.

MAKES ABOUT 2½ DOZEN COOKIES

In a stand mixer fitted with the paddle attachment, combine all the dry ingredients except the oats and the raisins. Add the butter and mix on low speed until blended. Add the eggs, egg whites, and vanilla and mix on medium-high speed until light and fluffy. Stir in the raisins and oats until blended. Cover and refrigerate for at least 2 hours or overnight.

Position a rack in the center of the oven. Preheat the oven to 350°F. Line two baking sheets with parchment paper or silicone baking mats.

Using a 1½-inch-diameter ice-cream scoop, drop mounds of batter 2 inches apart on the prepared pans. Bake one pan at a time for 18 to 20 minutes, or until the cookies are lightly browned. Remove from the oven and let the cookies cool on the pan for 5 minutes before transferring them to a wire rack to cool completely.

These cookies store nicely in an airtight container for up to 1 week.

BLACKBIRD BAKING TIP

If you prefer a flatter oatmeal-raisin cookie, just reduce the amount of gluten-free oats to 2 cups. Both ways are moist and oh-so-satisfying.

INGREDIENTS

- 1¼ cups packed light brown sugar
- ½ cup granulated sugar
- ½ cup sorghum flour
- ½ cup cornstarch
- ½ cup glutinous rice flour
- ½ teaspoon kosher salt
- 1¼ teaspoons ground cinnamon
- 2 teaspoons guar gum
- ½ teaspoon baking powder
- ¾ cup (1½ sticks) unsalted butter at room temperature
- 2 large eggs
- 2 large egg whites
- 2½ teaspoons pure vanilla extract
- 1½ cup raisins
- 2¼ cups gluten-free oats

molasses-spice cookies

- ½ cup (1 stick) plus 2 tablespoons unsalted butter, diced
- 1½ teaspoon grated fresh ginger
- 1½ cups sugar
- ¼ cup Brer Rabbit blackstrap molasses
- 2 large eggs, beaten
- ⅔ cup plus ½ cup tapioca flour
- ½ cup sorghum flour
- ½ cup cornstarch
- ¼ cup glutinous rice flour
- 2½ teaspoons guar gum
- ¾ teaspoon kosher salt
- 2 teaspoons baking soda
- 1 teaspoon ground cinnamon
- ½ teaspoon ground cardamom

The beauty of these cookies is that they are simultaneously crunchy and soft, which to me is the perfect texture for just about any cookie. This recipe is an adaption of a Carol Walters recipe, and they are loaded with seasonal spices, making them the ideal way to say "I love you" during the holidays and the cold winter months. These cookies are so fantastic that the husband of one of my customers came by with her to pick up an order, just to "meet the lady that made 'those crack cookies.'" Personally, I've never been more flattered in all my days of baking.

MAKES ABOUT 3 DOZEN COOKIES

In a large, heavy saucepan, melt the butter over low heat just until liquid. Remove from the heat and add the ginger. Let stand for 10 minutes. Whisk in 1 cup of the sugar and all the molasses until smooth. Add the eggs and whisk until smooth. In a medium bowl, combine the remaining dry ingredients, including the spices, and stir with a whisk to blend. Gradually stir the dry ingredients into the butter mixture until smooth. Cover and refrigerate for at least 2 hours or up to 1 day.

Position an oven rack in the center of the oven. Preheat the oven to 325°F. Line two baking sheets with parchment paper or silicone baking mats.

Pour the remaining ½ cup sugar into a shallow bowl or pie pan. Spoon out tablespoons of dough and roll them into balls between your palms. Roll the balls in the sugar, being sure to coat them evenly. Arrange the balls of dough 1½ inches apart on the prepared pans. Bake one pan at a time for 8 minutes, or until the cookies are flat, sugar-coated, and golden at the edges. Do not overbake, or the cookies will be too crisp. Remove from the oven and allow to cool on the pan for 5 minutes before transferring to a wire rack to cool completely.

These cookies keep very well in an airtight container for up to 2 weeks.

BLACKBIRD BAKING TIP

Different kinds of molasses have different pH balances. The pH balance matters greatly in this recipe as you want just the right pH to allow the baking soda to do its work. To my consternation, I found that the only molasses that worked for these cookies was Brer Rabbit; fortunately, it is widely available (see Resources if for some reason you can't find it).

rosa's coconut-date macaroons

This recipe came down to me from my Grandma Suhm. The first time I tried this recipe, I stood stock-still in my kitchen, eyes rolling back in my head. I was speechless. Shredded coconut, sweet Texas pecans, and Medjool dates suspended in meringue: Each bite is like a fairy tale come true. Often, people tell me that they don't even like coconut but they love these macaroons, and to me, that's all they have to say. You can never eat just one, and they are the perfect treat to end a meal, to enjoy with your afternoon espresso, or to give to that special someone. And they are always on the table at my house during the holidays.

INGREDIENTS

4 large egg whites

1 cup sugar

1½ teaspoons cornstarch

1¼ teaspoons pure vanilla extract

¾ teaspoon distilled white vinegar

2 tablespoons boiling water

1 cup chopped dried Medjool dates

1 cup finely chopped pecans

3 cups sweetened shredded coconut

MAKES ABOUT 3 DOZEN COOKIES

Position an oven rack in the center of the oven. Preheat the oven to 350°F. Line two baking sheets with parchment paper or silicone baking mats.

Using a stand electric mixer fitted with the whisk attachment, beat the egg whites on high speed until opaque and foamy.

In a small bowl, combine the sugar and cornstarch; stir with a small whisk to blend. Reduce the mixer speed to medium-low and gradually add the sugar mixture; mix for about 30 seconds, gradually bringing the mixer back to high speed and mix for 1 minute.

Immediately add the vanilla and vinegar and continue to mix for at least 2 minutes, or until the egg whites hold stiff, glossy peaks, stopping to scrape down the sides of the bowl once or twice.

Reduce the speed to medium-high and add the boiling water all at once. The egg whites will swell up and then resettle as all the water is incorporated. Mix for 2 minutes more, then set aside.

In a medium bowl, combine the dates, pecans, and coconut; using your hands, toss the ingredients until evenly distributed. This helps to avoid clumping, which can cause the egg whites to break down a bit too much due to overstirring.

Gently fold the coconut mixture into the egg white mixture until blended. Using a 1½-inch-diameter ice-cream scoop, place scoops of batter 1 inch apart on the prepared pans. Bake one sheet at a time for 8 minutes, then reduce the oven temperature to 225°F and bake for 40 minutes longer, or until the macaroons are an even light brown.

Remove from the oven and let cool on the pan for 15 minutes. Transfer the cookies to wire racks to cool completely.

Store in an airtight container in a cool, dry place for up to 1 week.

maraschino-marzipan kisses

This is one of the recipes that came down to me from my little Italian grandmother, Giovanna. During the holidays, she would always send my family tins filled with a variety of cookies and these were my favorites. Plus, I love to watch others enjoy these kisses because the look on their faces is priceless when they discover the unexpected cherry in the middle.

INGREDIENTS

2 cups almond flour

¾ cup sugar

2 large egg whites

⅜ teaspoon pure almond extract

2 cups (8 ounces) sliced almonds, coarsely crushed

one 1-pound jar maraschino cherries, drained

MAKES ABOUT 18 COOKIES

Position an oven rack in the center of the oven. Preheat the oven to 375°F. Line two baking sheets with parchment paper or silicone baking mats.

In a stand mixer fitted with the paddle attachment or a food processor, combine the almond flour and sugar and mix on low speed for a few seconds. Add the egg whites and almond extract and mix on high speed until the dough pulls together into a sticky mass and forms a ball. The dough should be firm. If it is very soft to the touch, add a couple of tablespoons of additional almond flour, mixing well.

Put the almonds in a pie pan. Using a 1¼-inch-diameter ice-cream scoop, scoop out the dough and transfer it to a flat surface; you should have about 18 balls of dough.

Fill a shallow bowl half-full with water and lightly wet the palm of one hand. Rub your hands together so that they are very lightly moist.

Take one of the dough balls and place it in the palm of your non-dominant hand. Gently press the ball into a disk the size of a half-dollar. Place a single cherry in the middle of the disk and then carefully lift the edges of the disk up and around the cherry, enrobing it in the dough. Roll the cookie between your hands to form a ball. If the dough pulls away from the cherry, your hands are too sticky, so lightly moisten them in the water again and then proceed. Roll the finished ball in the crushed almonds until evenly coated and place on one of the prepared pans. Repeat until all the cookies have been made.

Bake one pan at a time for 10 minutes, rotating the pan halfway through. The kisses are done when golden brown and faintly cracked on the surface. Remove from the oven and let the cookies cool on the pan for 5 minutes before transferring them to a wire rack to cool completely.

Store in an airtight container for up to 1½ weeks.

madeleines

Strange as it may seem, my inspiration for wanting to make madeleines came not from the culinary need to understand and conquer the task. It came to me as I gazed, transfixed, at Giorgio de Chirico's *Portrait Prémonitoire de Guillaume Apollinaire,* 1914, while touring the Pompidou Museum in Paris during the summer of 2006. A great white monolith carved with a fish and a madeleine appears to the right of the bust of an equally dominant man wearing sunglasses. The French poet, writer, and critic Apollinaire (1880–1918) has been credited with coining the word *surrealism.* Because metaphysical painting and surrealism are two of my favorite movements in the art world, I felt that this painting was a sign that I simply had to make these classic French treats gluten-free.

MAKES 12 MADELEINES

Note: For this recipe, you will need a twelve-mold madeleine pan, which can be found in kitchenware shops.

In a small bowl, combine the sorghum flour, cornstarch, tapioca flour, baking powder, and guar gum and stir with a whisk to blend. Using a stand mixer fitted with the whisk attachment, beat together the eggs, sugar, and orange flower water on high speed until thick enough to form a slowly dissolving ribbon on the surface when the beaters are lifted, about 5 minutes.

Sprinkle one-third of the dry ingredients over the egg mixture. Using a rubber spatula, gently fold in the dry ingredients until blended. Repeat to fold in the remaining dry ingredients in two increments. Pour in the melted butter and gently fold into the mixture. Fold in the lemon zest. Cover and refrigerate for 30 minutes.

Position an oven rack in the center of the oven. Preheat the oven to 425°F. Generously butter a 12-mold madeleine pan; dust with glutinous rice flour and knock out the excess flour. Place the pan on a baking sheet.

Spoon the batter into the prepared mold until three-fourths full. Bake for 8 to 10 minutes, or until lightly browned on the edges.

Remove from the oven and let cool in the pan for 5 minutes. Unmold onto wire racks to cool completely.

Store in an airtight container for up to 3 days.

INGREDIENTS

2½ tablespoons sorghum flour

2½ tablespoons cornstarch

1 tablespoon tapioca flour

¾ teaspoon baking powder

1¼ teaspoons guar gum

3 large eggs

½ cup sugar

1¼ teaspoons orange flower water

6 tablespoons unsalted butter, melted and cooled, plus more butter for the pan

zest of 1 Meyer lemon

glutinous rice flour for dusting

ladyfingers

- 4 large eggs, separated
- ½ cup granulated sugar, plus 1 tablespoon
- 1½ teaspoons pure vanilla extract
- ¼ cup sorghum flour
- ⅓ cup cornstarch
- ¼ cup tapioca flour
- 1 teaspoon baking powder
- 1 teaspoon guar gum
- ⅛ teaspoon salt
- ½ cup confectioners' sugar, sifted

Mastering the ladyfingers recipe opened the door to all the more complicated recipes I'd been dying to make but couldn't because I lacked this key ingredient. These are standard for snack time and essential for layered desserts, like charlottes and tiramisù.

MAKES 12 LADYFINGERS

Position an oven rack in the center of the oven. Preheat the oven to 350°F. Line two jellyroll pans with parchment paper or silicone baking mats.

In a stand mixer fitted with the whisk attachment, beat the egg yolks with the ½ cup granulated sugar on high speed until a slowly dissolving ribbon is formed on the surface when the beaters are lifted. Fold in the vanilla. In a clean bowl with clean beaters, beat the egg whites until stiff peaks form; add the 1 tablespoon granulated sugar and whisk for about 30 seconds more, or until the peaks are glossy.

In a small bowl, combine the sorghum flour, cornstarch, tapioca flour, baking powder, guar gum, and salt and stir with a whisk to blend. In three separate batches, sprinkle the dry ingredients over the egg whites and gently fold in with a rubber spatula. Repeat with the egg yolk mixture. Spoon the batter into a pastry bag fitted with a 1-inch plain pastry tip. Pipe 4½-inch-long fingers 1 inch apart on the prepared pans. You should have 12 fingers. Dust with confectioners' sugar and bake one pan at a time for 20 minutes, or until the cookies are firm and lightly browned.

Remove from the oven. Transfer the cookies to a wire rack to cool completely. Repeat to cook the remaining batter.

Store in an airtight container for up to 1 week.

BLACKBIRD BAKING TIP

If you'd like to save time, ladyfinger pans are available and extremely easy to use. Just spray each mold with non-stick spray before you fill them with batter.

chia and poppy seed shortbread with pomegranate glaze

I first discovered chia seeds while doing research on celiac disease, and I was so fascinated that I immediately pulled them into my pantry. In these shortbread squares, the nutty flavor of the chia seeds pairs seamlessly with the sweet crunch of the poppy seeds, while the buttery cookie is given the contrast of a bright pomegranate glaze.

MAKES 12 SQUARES

Position an oven rack in the center of the oven. Preheat the oven to 350°F. Line a small jellyroll pan with aluminum foil, letting the aluminum foil overlap two sides of the pan. Lightly spray the foil with nonstick cooking spray.

In a stand mixer fitted with the paddle attachment, combine all the dry ingredients and mix on low speed to blend. Add the butter and mix on low speed until the mixture resembles coarse bread crumbs. Add the eggs and vanilla and almond extracts and mix on medium-high speed until the dough begins to pull from the sides of the bowl. Mix on high speed for 10 seconds. Using a rubber spatula, fold in the chia and poppy seeds. Transfer the dough to the prepared pan and spread evenly using an offset spatula. Bake for 25 minutes, or until just beginning to color. Remove from the oven, transfer the pan to a wire rack, and let cool completely.

Lift the shortbread from the pan by holding onto the sides of the aluminum foil. Remove the aluminum foil and use a large, sharp knife to cut the shortbread into 3-inch squares. Decorate each square by piping on the glaze in a crisscross pattern. Allow the glaze to set for about 10 minutes before serving.

Store in an airtight container for up to 3 days.

ABOUT CHIA SEEDS

For thousands of years, chia seeds were prized in Mesoamerica for their stamina-building properties. They were so valued by the Aztecs that they were used as a form of tribute to the priests and nobles. Chia seeds can retain twelve times their weight in water, prolonging hydration and making them an ideal "runner's food." Additionally, these little seeds are a potent source of omega-3 fatty acids, easily digestible proteins, vitamins, minerals, and soluble fiber, making them, to me, a super food. Chia seeds can be found at most natural foods stores and should be stored in a cool, dry place.

INGREDIENTS

- 1 cup millet flour
- ½ cup sorghum flour
- ½ cup cornstarch
- ½ cup tapioca flour
- ¼ cup golden baker's sugar
- ¾ cup granulated sugar
- 2½ teaspoons guar gum
- 1 teaspoon baking powder
- ¼ teaspoon kosher salt
- 1 cup (2 sticks) cold, unsalted butter, diced
- 2 large eggs
- 1½ teaspoons pure vanilla extract
- 1½ teaspoons pure almond extract
- 1½ tablespoons chia seeds (see Note)
- 1½ tablespoons poppy seeds
- Pomegranate Glaze (page 66)

Special equipment:
  Ateco plain stainless steel tip No. 5

pomegranate glaze

MAKES ¼ CUP

3   tablespoons bottled pomegranate juice

1   cup confectioners' sugar, sifted

1   tablespoon light corn syrup

zest of ½ lemon

In a medium bowl, whisk together the pomegranate juice and confectioners' sugar. Add the corn syrup and the lemon zest and whisk until smooth. Transfer the thick glaze to a pastry bag fitted with a small plain tip.

almond biscotti, two ways

These cookies own an opulent room in my heart, as they were my beloved grandmother's favorite little treat. A spitfire in a four-foot-ten Italian frame, Giovanna was just as particular about her little treats as she was about the level of cleanliness of her little house. She worked harder than anyone I have ever known, but when she did decide to take a breather, these were the cookies she dunked in her afternoon coffee while chatting on the phone with her friends.

MAKES 3 DOZEN BISCOTTI

Position an oven rack in the center of the oven. Preheat the oven to 375°F. Line two baking sheets with parchment paper or silicone baking mats.

On a large pastry board, combine all the dry ingredients and mix with a dough scraper to blend. Make a well in the center and add 3 of the eggs, being careful not to allow any bits of shell to fall in. Add the almond extract and ¼ teaspoon of the vanilla extract.

Using a steady folding motion with the pastry scraper, begin pulling the dry ingredients from the side of the well into the liquid center. If the mass spreads out, push it back together with your hands. If the sides of the mass break, just keep folding everything back into the center. Continue to mix until the ingredients are blended and form a ball. Scrape the dough from the pastry board, dust the board with tapioca flour, and then knead the dough several more times until smooth. Flatten the dough, sprinkle with the almonds, and knead again until they are evenly distributed. Divide the dough in half with a large knife.

Set one half of the dough aside. Dust the pastry board with additional tapioca flour and flatten the second piece of dough on the board. Add the cocoa powder, the remaining ½ teaspoon vanilla, and the remaining egg. Knead until very smooth, then add the chocolate chips, being careful to knead just until smooth. The dough should be firm and soft at this point, but not overly dry. If the dough "cracks" when pressed, add water, 1 tablespoon at a time, until the dough feels supple. Cut each piece of dough in half, then carefully shape each of the 4 pieces into a 12-inch-long log. Place two logs 3 inches apart on each of the prepared pans and slightly flatten each log.

continued

1½ cups sorghum flour

1   cup cornstarch

½   cup almond meal

⅛   teaspoon kosher salt

1   teaspoon baking soda

2   teaspoons guar gum

1   cup granulated sugar

4   large eggs

2½ teaspoons pure almond extract

¾   teaspoon pure vanilla extract

tapioca flour for dusting

½   cup slivered almonds, coarsely chopped

⅓   cup unsweetened cocoa powder

¼   cup semisweet chocolate chips

1   large egg white, lightly beaten

sanding sugar for sprinkling

1 to 3 tablespoons lukewarm water, if needed

Brush each log with egg white and sprinkle with the sanding sugar. Bake for 20 minutes, rotating the pans front to back and from the top rack to the bottom. Biscotti are done when the dough has cracked on top. Remove from the oven and transfer one log to a cutting board; leave the oven on, but reduce the oven temperature to 225°F. Using a serrated knife, cut the log into ½-inch-thick diagonal slices. Lay the cookies flat when you return them to the baking sheet and bake for 30 minutes, or until they are lightly golden.

Remove from the oven. Transfer the cookies to wire racks to cool completely.

Store in an airtight container for up to 2 weeks.

- 1 cup (2 sticks) unsalted butter

- 4 ounces high-quality unsweetened chocolate, such as Scharffen Berger, chopped

- 2 ounces high-quality bittersweet chocolate, such as Scharffen Berger, chopped

- 2 cups sugar

- ¼ cup almond meal

- ½ cup cornstarch

- ¼ cup tapioca flour

- ¼ cup glutinous rice flour

- 1¾ teaspoons guar gum

- 1 teaspoon kosher salt

- 5 large eggs

- 2½ teaspoons pure vanilla extract

brownies for lovers

One of the first baked goods that I made repeatedly as a teenager and later devoted long hours of experimentation to as I began my journey into the gluten-free world was the brownie. Everyone has his or her own interpretation of a good brownie, and mine is one with a slightly chewy edge and a soft, but not too soft, center, falling just between the chewy and cakey varieties. To achieve this goal, it's important to use the freshest possible eggs and the highest-quality chocolate you can get your hands on.

These brownies are for anyone who believes that love at first bite is still possible.

MAKES 16 BROWNIES

Position an oven rack in the center of the oven. Preheat the oven to 350°F. Take a piece of parchment paper and using a pair of kitchen scissors, cut 2 inches into each corner (right where the two edges of the paper meet) at a 45° angle. Press the parchment into the greased 9-by-13-inch pan. The slits you cut into the corners will allow you to fit the paper into the pan with perfectly smooth edges.

In a large stainless-steel bowl set over a saucepan with 2 inches of barely simmering water (don't let the bowl touch the water), melt the butter and chocolate, being careful not to let the chocolate scorch. Whisk in 1 cup of the sugar. Remove from the heat and set aside.

In a medium bowl, combine all the dry ingredients and stir with a whisk to blend. Set aside.

Using a stand mixer fitted with the whisk attachment, whisk the eggs with the remaining 1 cup sugar until the eggs have doubled in volume. Stir half of the egg mixture into the melted chocolate mixture, then stir in half of the dry ingredients. Repeat this process and stir until the batter looks like chocolate pudding. Fold in the vanilla. Pour the batter into the prepared pan, smooth the top, and bake for 30 minutes, or until the brownies are cracked around the edges.

Remove from the oven and let cool completely in the pan on a wire rack. Lift the brownies out by grasping the two sides of the parchment paper. Transfer to a cutting board and remove the paper. Cut into 16 bars.

Store in an airtight container for up to 3 days and for up to 1 week in the refrigerator.

meyer lemon bars

During the summer and into the fall, my family always seemed to have an abundance of lemon bars around the house, and my mother made the best I've ever had. The slight salt of the crust coupled with the sweet and sour of the lemon curd was a meditation on opposites that resonated deeply with me, even then. I remember thinking, with each successive bite, "How in the hell did she *do* that?" It was like a form of magic, and I wanted so badly to emulate that. Truth be told, it was the lemon bar that awakened that curious seeker within me, all those years ago, so I absolutely could not leave it out of my collection. Hopefully these will have the same impact on your taste buds as they do on mine.

Although this recipe calls for Meyer lemons, which have a thinner skin and sweeter juice than regular lemons, you can use regular lemons for an equally mouthwatering result.

MAKES 16 BARS

Position an oven rack in the center of the oven. Preheat the oven to 350°F. Lightly butter an 9-by-9-inch baking pan.

For the crust: In a stand mixer fitted with the paddle attachment, cream the butter together with the brown sugar until light and fluffy. Add the rest of the dry ingredients and beat until the mixture resembles small peas. Add the eggs and beat until the dough folds in on itself.

Spray your hands with nonstick cooking spray and press the dough into the prepared pan until even. Bake for 15 minutes, or until the crust just begins to pull away from the sides of the pan and the edges are golden brown.

For the lemon curd: While the crust is baking, in a medium stainless-steel saucepan, combine the sugar and cornstarch. Stir with a whisk to blend. Whisk in the eggs and lemon juice until very smooth. Add the lemon zest and the butter. Set the saucepan over a medium flame. Stirring constantly, cook the curd just until it boils. Whisk vigorously and then remove from the heat, about 10 seconds.

continued

INGREDIENTS

Crust

- 12 tablespoons salted butter at room temperature, plus more for greasing pan
- ¼ cup light brown sugar
- ½ cup sorghum flour
- ½ cup glutinous rice flour
- ½ cup cornstarch
- 1½ teaspoons guar gum
- 2 eggs

Meyer Lemon Curd

- 1½ cups granulated sugar
- ¼ cup cornstarch
- 8 large eggs, beaten
- zest of 2 Meyer lemons
- 1¼ cups fresh Meyer lemon juice
- 6 tablespoons unsalted butter
- confectioners' sugar for dusting

Remove the hot crust from the oven and immediately pour the hot lemon curd onto it. Smooth the top and return to the oven; cook for 15 minutes, or until the edges of the curd just begin to pull away from the sides of the pan. Remove from the oven and let cool completely in the pan on a wire rack. Cut into sixteen 2½-inch bars. Dust with confectioners' sugar before serving.

Store in an airtight container in a cool, dry place for up to 3 days.

BLACKBIRD BAKING TIP

Don't refrigerate the lemon bars, as this will cause condensation to form, making the confectioners' sugar dissolve on impact.

millet and honey graham cracker s'mores

Coming up with this graham cracker recipe was like opening a box filled with pictures from my childhood. It made me remember how my brothers and sisters and I would get into an absolute frenzy to make s'mores—so much so that we would roast the marshmallows over the blue flame on our mother's gas stove rather than wait for the fire to be built.

These sublimely simple graham crackers topped with molten marshmallows and milk chocolate are just as fun to make at home as around the campfire, but make sure you roast the marshmallows low and slow for the perfect melt.

MAKES TWELVE 5-BY-4-INCH GRAHAM CRACKERS AND 6 S'MORES

For the graham crackers: In a stand mixer fitted with the paddle attachment, combine all the dry ingredients, including the sugars, and mix on low speed to blend. Add the butter and mix on low speed until blended. Add the eggs, honey, and vanilla. Increase the mixer speed to medium-high and mix until the dough forms a ball.

Transfer the dough to a work surface lightly dusted with rice flour. Knead the dough a few times until smooth.

Using a large knife, divide the dough into four sections. Shape each section into a flat rectangle. Cover in plastic wrap and refrigerate for at least 13 hours or up to 2 days.

Position an oven rack in the center of the oven. Preheat the oven to 350°F. Line two baking sheets with parchment paper or silicone baking mats.

Dust the work surface again with glutinous rice flour and roll one piece of the dough out to a 5-by-12-inch rectangle. Using a very sharp chef's knife, trim the edges so they are perfectly straight. Cut the dough into three 5-by-4-inch rectangles. Transfer the dough to a prepared pan and perforate the tops of each rectangle with a wooden skewer. Repeat with the remaining pieces of dough.

Bake one pan at a time for 13 to 15 minutes, or until lightly browned on the edges.

Remove from the oven. Transfer the cookies to a wire rack to cool completely. Repeat to cook the remaining cookies.

continued

INGREDIENTS

Graham Crackers

- 2½ cups millet flour
- 1¾ cups plus 2 tablespoons glutinous rice flour
- 2 tablespoons amaranth flour
- 1 teaspoon ground cinnamon
- 1 teaspoon baking soda
- 1 teaspoon kosher salt
- 4 teaspoons guar gum
- ⅔ cup packed light brown sugar
- ½ cup granulated sugar
- 1½ cups (3 sticks) cold unsalted butter, diced
- 4 large eggs
- ¼ cup honey
- 2 tablespoons pure vanilla extract

Filling

- one 1-pound bag air-puffed marshmallows
- 6 milk chocolate bars

millet and honey graham cracker s'mores, continued

For the filling: Pierce 2 marshmallows with a wooden-handled long fork or barbecue fork and hold them over a low open flame, rotating constantly until they are evenly browned and wrinkled.

Place half of one chocolate bar on top of a graham cracker. Immediately layer the marshmallows over the chocolate and top with another graham cracker.

Repeat to make the remaining s'mores. Serve immediately.

The graham crackers will keep for up to 2 weeks in a airtight container.

millet power bars

Although I am a baker and adore desserts, I'm also a bit of a health nut and an avid practitioner of yoga. So, I wanted to come up with the most healthful power bar possible. Packed with a superabundance of nutrition, these bars are high in protein thanks to the millet and brown rice, loaded with omega-3s thanks to the almonds, and teeming with antioxidants thanks to the dried blueberries and cherries.

MAKES 12 BARS

Lightly coat a jellyroll pan with nonstick cooking spray and set aside.

Set a large stainless-steel bowl over a saucepan filled with 4 inches of simmering water (don't let the bottom of the bowl touch the water). Add the butter and honey to the bowl and melt the butter. Stir to blend. Add the marshmallows and stir to coat each one evenly. This will encourage the marshmallows to melt more evenly, and thus more rapidly. Cook, stirring every 5 minutes or so, until the marshmallows have melted, 20 to 25 minutes.

While you are waiting for the marshmallows to transform, combine the two kinds of almonds and the dried fruit in a medium bowl and stir to blend. Combine the puffed rice and millet in a large bowl and stir to blend.

When the marshmallows have melted completely, remove the bowl from the pan, being careful of the steam. Place it on a kitchen towel on a large work surface. Add the cereal and the dried fruit and nuts to the marshmallows. Spray your hands with nonstick cooking spray and begin mixing the ingredients together until blended; the marshmallows should not be so hot that they burn your hands but still warm and melted. Using a plastic dough scraper, transfer the sticky mass to the prepared pan. Spray a rolling pin with nonstick cooking spray.

Press the ingredients as evenly as possible into the pan with your hands. Take the rolling pin and press on the mixture, going from the corner of one end to the opposite corner on the other end. Now, do the same thing beginning with the other corner. Roll down the center of the pan several times until it is perfectly flat. Loosely cover the pan with plastic wrap and let the mixture stand for at least 15 minutes or up to 24 hours. Insert a metal spatula between the bars and the edges to release from the pan. Unmold the bars by inverting on to a cutting board. Using a serrated knife, cut into 12 bars.

Wrap in plastic wrap and store in an airtight container for up to 2 weeks.

INGREDIENTS

nonstick cooking spray

1½ tablespoons unsalted butter

1 tablespoon orange blossom honey

one 1-pound bag air-puffed marshmallows

1 cup sliced almonds

1 cup slivered almonds

1¼ cups dried sour cherries

1¼ cups dried blueberries

5 cups puffed brown rice cereal, such as Arrowhead Mills

5 cups puffed millet cereal, such as Arrowhead Mills

CHAPTER THREE

tarts, pies & cobblers

poires en croute with champagne crème anglaise

Although this recipe has many steps, the labor is well worth it, as this dessert is dressed to impress. The pears are hollowed out and filled with Cognac-soaked currants, orange zest, and sugar, then baked in a wine-infused pastry crust. Served in a bath of Champagne crème anglaise, they are the perfect ending to any meal. I recommend serving these cool in the summer and warm in the winter.

INGREDIENTS

- 1 disk Sweet Pâte Brisée (short crust dough; page 98), made with 1 egg and 2 tablespoons dry white wine
- 6 tablespoons dried currants
- 6 tablespoons Cognac
- 4 ripe but firm Bosc pears with stems, peeled
- 6 tablespoons sugar
- 4 teaspoons cornstarch
- ¾ teaspoon ground cinnamon
- 1½ teaspoons orange zest
- 4 tablespoons unsalted butter
- rice flour for dusting

Champagne Crème Anglaise

- 2 cups whole milk
- 1 vanilla bean, split lengthwise, or 1½ teaspoons pure vanilla extract
- ¼ cup sugar
- 6 large egg yolks
- 2 tablespoons Champagne

SERVES 4

Cover the disk of dough in plastic wrap and refrigerate overnight. In a small bowl, combine the currants and Cognac. Cover and refrigerate overnight. Remove the currants from the refrigerator and set aside.

Cut the pears in half crosswise where the bulbous base meets the base of the neck. Reserve the tops. Using a melon baller, make a hole in the top of each base and remove the core of the pear, working carefully to keep from splitting the pear open. Be sure to remove all the seeds and enough of the flesh for each pear to hold about 2 tablespoons of filling. Carefully level the pears by cutting the bottoms evenly flat. Set aside.

In a small bowl, combine the sugar, cornstarch, and cinnamon. Stir with a small whisk to blend. Pour the soaked currants into a heavy, medium saucepan and add the orange zest. Add the dry ingredients and stir to coat the currants evenly. Finally, add the butter and turn the heat to medium-low. Cook, stirring constantly, until the mixture comes to a rolling boil, about 3 minutes. Remove from the heat and set aside. The mixture will thicken as it cools.

Remove the dough from the refrigerator and remove the plastic wrap; let stand for 15 minutes. Position an oven rack in the center of the oven and preheat the oven to 375°F.

Dust a work surface with rice flour and roll out the dough to a 14-inch square. Cut the dough into four 7-inch squares. Fill the cored base of a pear with about 2 tablespoons of the filling. Cap with the reserved top. Repeat to fill and cap all the pears.

continued

Set a pear in the center of one of the pastry squares. Brush the edges of the dough with water and carefully gather the dough up around the stem of the pear, one corner at a time, and trim the excess dough where there is significant overlap. Smooth out the seams of the dough by dipping your fingers in a bowl of water and running over the overlap until it binds to the dough underneath.

Repeat until all of the pears are covered. Carefully transfer the pears to a roasting pan and bake for 25 minutes, or until the dough begins to take on color just beneath the stems of the pears.

Remove from the oven and let cool in the pan for 20 minutes before serving.

Meanwhile, for the crème anglaise: In a small, heavy saucepan, combine the milk and vanilla bean (if using). Cook over medium-low heat until bubbles form around the edges of the pan. Using a whisk or a stand mixer fitted with the whisk attachment, beat together the sugar and egg yolks until thick enough to form a slowly dissolving ribbon on the surface when the beaters are lifted. Whisk about ½ cup of the hot milk into the egg mixture. Gradually whisk in the remaining milk. Return to the pan and cook, stirring constantly, over medium heat until the custard is thick enough to coat the back of a wooden spoon. When you run your finger down the back of the spoon you should leave a trail. Do not overcook; this is a thin custard. Immediately remove from the heat and stir in the vanilla extract (if using), along with the Champagne. Strain through a fine-mesh sieve into a bowl; remove the vanilla bean.

Use now, or let cool, cover with a sheet of plastic wrap pressed directly onto the surface, and refrigerate for up to 2 days.

To serve, pour about ⅓ cup crème anglaise into each of 4 shallow bowls. Place a pear in the center of each bowl.

strawberry tartlets with vanilla pastry cream

These tartlets were inspired by the fruit itself, but also by an indelible memory from my time living and cooking at a château in Nans-Sous-Sainte-Anne, France. Covering the stone wall just across the street from the château were wild strawberries. They were little things, no bigger than the fingernail on my pinky finger, but so intensely flavorful that tasting them was like being read the most precise definition of what "strawberry" flavor really was.

My son, Leo, and I devoured them. Hand over fist, we plucked those crimson fruits, each one tasting better than the last, and I've never tasted anything as intoxicating since.

MAKES 6 TARTLETS

Position an oven rack in the center of the oven. Preheat the oven to 400°F. Remove both disks of dough from the refrigerator and let stand for 15 minutes before rolling them out.

Dust a work surface with tapioca flour and begin rolling out one disk of dough to a thickness of ¼ inch, rotating and turning often to insure an even surface. Using a 5-inch round pastry cutter, cut out three rounds. Fit each round into a 4-inch tart pan with a removable bottom, pressing it into the sides. Run the rolling pin over the top of the pan to trim the dough. Repeat with the second disk of dough to make a total of six tartlets. Pierce the bottom of the pastry in each pan with a fork. Place the pans on a baking sheet.

Bake for 13 to 15 minutes, or until the crusts are lightly colored. Remove from the oven and transfer to wire racks to let the tart cases cool completely.

For the pastry cream: In a heavy, medium saucepan, heat the half-and-half over medium-low heat until bubbles form around the edges of the pan; do not simmer. Remove from the heat. In a medium bowl, combine the egg yolks, 4 tablespoons sugar, and cornstarch and whisk until thick and pale in color. Gradually whisk the hot half-and-half into the egg yolk mixture. Return to the pan and cook over medium heat, whisking constantly, until thick enough to coat the back of a wooden spoon. Stir in the vanilla and immediately transfer to a bowl. Cover with plastic wrap pressed directly onto the surface of the custard to prevent a skin from forming. Refrigerate for at least 30 minutes or up to 2 days.

continued

2 disks Sweet Pâte Brisée (short crust dough; page 98)

tapioca flour for dusting

Pastry Cream

1¼ cups half-and-half

4 large egg yolks

4 tablespoons sugar

¼ cup cornstarch

1 teaspoon pure vanilla extract

⅓ cup strawberry preserves

¼ teaspoon lemon juice

2 cups fresh strawberries, hulled

1¼ cups heavy cream

1½ tablespoons sugar

mint sprigs for garnish

strawberry tartlets with vanilla pastry cream, continued

In a small saucepan, melt the strawberry preserves over low heat. Stir in the lemon juice. Strain the preserves through a fine-mesh sieve and set aside.

Remove the sides of the tart pans and place the tart cases on a wire rack. Whisk the pastry cream to insure its smoothness and spoon into the tart cases, filling them three-fourths full to allow room for the strawberries. Place the strawberries on top of the cream. Brush the strained preserves over the berries.

In a deep bowl, beat the heavy cream with an electric mixer until soft peaks form. Beat in the 1½ tablespoons sugar, mixing for just a few seconds. Garnish each tartlet with a dollop of cream and a mint sprig.

Serve now or refrigerate for up to 1 day. These are best served the day they are made.

tarte tatin

The first time I tried a traditional tarte Tatin, it wasn't beneath a Parisian canopy on a beautifully named street in the City of Light. It was smack dab in the middle of downtown Austin, Texas, in the early fall of 2001, before my diagnosis and before I was married. But the man who presented this bit of culinary genius to me was none other than Tim Morgan, the man I would eventually marry, and as he unveiled the tart, he quietly said, "I'm not much of a baker, but this is my favorite."

It was the most incredible tart I had ever placed in my mouth. The succulently tender caramelized apples nestled in the ever so slightly sweet dough, and topped with a dollop of crème fraîche, were a revelation.

MAKES ONE 12-INCH TART; SERVES 10

For the dough: In a stand mixer fitted with the paddle attachment, combine all the dry ingredients and mix on low speed to blend. Add the cultured butter and continue to mix on low speed until the mixture resembles coarse bread crumbs. Add the egg and mix on medium-high until the dough turns in on itself. Turn out the dough onto a surface dusted with rice flour and knead for several turns. Wrap in plastic wrap and refrigerate for at least 2 hours or up to 2 days.

In a 12-inch ovenproof skillet or tarte Tatin pan, evenly arrange the diced unsalted butter over the bottom of the pan and top with the granulated sugar. Arrange the apples on their sides, with all the cored sides facing the same direction, in a tight concentric circle. The pan should be snugly packed.

Place the pan over medium heat and cook for about 30 minutes, or until the apples are translucent and golden brown. Gently shake the pan every 10 minutes or so to keep the apples from sticking. Just before the apples are done, remove the dough from the fridge and remove the plastic wrap; let stand for 15 minutes. When the apples are done, remove from the heat and let cool until the dough has been rolled out.

Preheat the oven to 425°F. On a work surface dusted with tapioca flour, roll out the dough to a 14-inch-diameter round. Position the dough over the center of the pan and tuck the edges of the dough down inside the edges of the pan. Bake for about 30 minutes, or until golden brown.

The tart will be extremely hot, so be very careful removing it from the oven. Let cool on a wire rack for at least 5 minutes. Unmold onto a large plate.

Serve warm, with crème fraîche.

Refrigerate, lightly covered, for up to 3 days.

INGREDIENTS

Pâte Sucrée (sweet short pastry dough)

- ¾ cup plus 2 tablespoons tapioca flour, plus more for dusting
- ¾ cup cornstarch
- ¼ cup glutinous rice flour, plus more for dusting
- 6 tablespoons millet flour
- ⅛ teaspoon kosher salt
- 1½ teaspoons guar gum
- 1 cup confectioners' sugar
- 1 cup (2 sticks) cold unsalted cultured butter, diced
- 1 large egg, beaten

- ½ cup (1 stick) cold unsalted butter, diced
- 2 cups granulated sugar
- 13 Golden Delicious apples, peeled, halved, and cored

crème fraîche for serving

frangipane tart with blueberries and red currants

INGREDIENTS

1 recipe Pâte Sucrée (sweet
   short pastry dough; page 89)

tapioca flour for dusting

Frangipane Filling

3 large egg yolks

¼ cup sugar

3 tablespoons plus 1 teaspoon
   cornstarch

1 cup whole milk

¼ cup almond meal

2 tablespoons unsalted butter

1½ tablespoons Amaretto
   liqueur

2 cups fresh blueberries

1 cup fresh red currants

½ cup red currant jelly

sweetened lightly whipped
   cream for serving

mint sprigs for garnish

The presentation of a fresh fruit tart is always breathtaking, and this one has the added bonus of fabulous taste. The sweet and sour bursts of fruit exploding between your teeth, the delicacy of the frangipane, and the flakiness of the crust culminate in a magnificent tart that is sure to garner an abundance of compliments.

SERVES 6

Position an oven rack in the center of the oven. Preheat the oven to 400°F. Remove the dough from the refrigerator and remove the plastic wrap at least 15 minutes before rolling out the dough.

On a work surface dusted with tapioca flour, roll out the dough to a 6-by-16-inch rectangle. Fit the dough into a 4-by-14-inch tart pan with a removable bottom and press the dough into the corners and sides of the pan. Run a rolling pin over the top of the pan to trim the dough. Roll the extra dough into a long rope the width of a pencil and nestle it into the crease of the pan for additional support. Smooth with your fingers and a few drops of water. Dock the bottom of the crust with a fork.

Bake for 12 minutes, or until the edges just begin to take on color. Remove from the oven and let cool completely in the pan on a wire rack.

For the filling: In a medium bowl, combine the egg yolks, sugar, and cornstarch. Using an electric mixer fitted with the whisk attachment, beat the egg yolk mixture on high speed until thickened enough that a slowly dissolving ribbon forms on the surface when the beaters are lifted.

In a small, heavy saucepan, heat the milk over medium-low heat until bubbles form around the edges of the pan. Gradually whisk the hot milk into the egg mixture. Return the mixture to the pan and cook over medium-low heat, whisking constantly, until the whisk leaves lines in the custard. Remove from the heat and whisk in the almond meal, butter, and Amaretto until smooth. If not using immediately, cover by pressing plastic wrap directly onto the surface of the frangipane. To store, let cool, then refrigerate for up to 12 hours.

Fill the crust with the frangipane and smooth the top with an offset spatula.

continued

frangipane tart with blueberries and red currants, continued

Top the frangipane first with the blueberries and then with the currants. In a small saucepan, heat the jelly over low heat until runny. Using a pastry brush, gently brush the fruit with the warm currant jelly, giving the fruit a glistening touch.

Cut into squares and serve topped with whipped cream and garnished with mint sprigs.

caramelized alsatian onion tart

This is the first savory tart I ever made; it was on a cooking trip to San Francisco, and everyone absolutely loved it. The onions are cooked twice, first in butter and then in chicken stock for a good two hours, making them so tender they literally melt in your mouth. The crisp bacon adds a salty, apple-smoked dimension, and the crust is flaky, buttery, and effusively light. Leave it on the counter overnight if there is anything left over, and try it for breakfast with a poached egg. "Oh my God," will be the resounding echo in your mind.

MAKES ONE 10-INCH TART; SERVES 6

Note: The crust recipe makes enough dough for two 10-inch tarts; freeze the extra dough for up to 1 month.

For the dough: In a stand mixer fitted with the paddle attachment, combine all the dry ingredients and mix on low speed to blend. Add the butter and beat until the mixture resembles coarse bread crumbs. Add the eggs and beat on medium speed until the dough turns in on itself and forms a sticky ball. Turn the dough out onto a work surface that has been lightly dusted with rice flour. Knead several times until smooth. Divide the dough in half, shape each into a disk, and wrap in plastic wrap. Refrigerate one disk of dough for at least 2 hours or up to 2 days; freeze the second disk of dough for up to 1 month for another use.

Position an oven rack in the center of the oven. Preheat the oven to 400°F. Remove the dough from the refrigerator and remove the plastic wrap 15 minutes before rolling out the dough. Dust a work surface with tapioca flour and roll out the dough into a 12-inch round.

Fit the dough into a 10-inch tart pan with a removable bottom and press it against the sides. Run the rolling pin over the top of the pan to trim the dough. Pierce the bottom of the crust half a dozen times with a fork. Partially bake for 10 minutes, or until golden about the edges. Remove from the oven and let cool completely in the pan on a wire rack. Turn off oven.

For the filling: In a large sauté pan, melt the butter over medium heat and add the onions. Cook, stirring frequently, for 20 to 30 minutes, or until golden brown. Season with salt and pepper. Add the chicken stock and reduce the heat to low. Cook, stirring occasionally, until all the liquid has evaporated, 1½ to 2 hours.

continued

INGREDIENTS

Pâte Brisée (short crust dough)

- ¾ cup plus 2 tablespoons glutinous rice flour, plus more for dusting
- ¾ cup cornstarch
- ¼ cup plus 2 tablespoons tapioca flour
- ¼ cup sorghum flour
- ⅛ teaspoon sugar
- ⅛ teaspoon kosher salt
- 1½ teaspoons guar gum
- 1 cup (2 sticks) cold unsalted cultured butter, diced
- 3 large eggs, beaten

Filling

- 4 tablespoons unsalted butter
- 4 large white onions, diced
- 2 teaspoons kosher salt
- 1 teaspoon freshly ground pepper
- 2 cups chicken stock
- 6 thick slices applewood-smoked bacon, cut into lardons (matchsticks)

fresh flat-leaf parsley leaves for garnish

caramelized alsatian onion tart, continued

In a medium skillet, sauté the bacon over medium heat until crisp. Using tongs or a slotted spoon, transfer the bacon to paper towels to drain. Reserve a couple of the lardons for garnish. Stir the rest of the bacon into the onions.

Preheat oven to 400°F. Fill the cooled tart shell with the onion mixture and smooth the top. Bake for 20 minutes, or until bubbling slightly about the edges. Let cool completely in the pan on a wire rack.

To serve, remove the sides of the pan and cut the tart into wedges. Garnish with the reserved lardons and a parsley leaf.

tapenade-tomato tart with buffalo mozzarella

The dough for this savory tart is made with a touch of goat butter, creating a subtle flavor that brings out the flavor of the tapenade in soft waves. The soft, creamy fresh buffalo mozzarella balances perfectly with the intensity of the garlic.

MAKES ONE 12-INCH TART; SERVES 8

Note: The crust recipe makes enough dough for two 12-inch tarts; freeze the extra dough for up to 1 month.

For the pâte brisée: In a stand mixer fitted with the paddle attachment, combine all the dry ingredients and mix on low speed to blend. Add the goat butter and the unsalted butter and mix on low speed until the mixture resembles coarse crumbs. Add the egg and mix on high speed until the mixture folds in on itself and forms a ball. Turn the dough out onto a surface dusted with tapioca flour and knead 3 or 4 times. Form into two disks, cover with plastic wrap, and refrigerate one disk of dough for at least 2 hours or up to 2 days; the second disk of dough may be frozen for up to 1 month for another use.

For the tapenade: In a food processor, combine the olives, anchovies, capers, and garlic. Pulse until the ingredients look uniform. With the machine running, gradually add the olive oil to make a thick paste. Scrape down the sides of the processor as necessary and pulse until smooth. Set aside.

Position an oven rack in the center of the oven. Preheat the oven to 400°F. Remove the dough from the refrigerator and remove the plastic wrap 15 minutes before rolling out the dough. On a work surface dusted with tapioca flour, roll out the dough to a 14-inch round. Fit the dough into a 12-inch tart pan with a removable bottom, pressing it into the sides of the pan. Run the rolling pin over the top of the pan to trim the dough. Bake the tart shell for 10 minutes. Remove from oven and immediately spread the tapenade in the bottom of the crust and smooth the top. Arrange the cheese and tomato slices alternately in a concentric pattern on top of the tapenade. Sprinkle the tart with the thyme and black pepper and bake for 15 minutes, or until the mozzarella is just beginning to brown. Remove from the oven and let cool on a wire rack. Remove the sides of the pan and cut the tart into wedges to serve.

INGREDIENTS

Goat Butter Pâte Brisée

- ½ cup tapioca flour, plus more for dusting
- ¾ cup millet flour
- ¼ cup sorghum flour
- ½ cup cornstarch
- ¼ cup glutinous rice flour
- ⅛ teaspoon kosher salt
- 1 tablespoon sugar
- 1½ teaspoons guar gum
- 2 tablespoons cold goat butter
- ¾ cup (1½ sticks) plus 2 tablespoons cold unsalted butter, diced
- 2 large eggs

Tapenade

- ½ cup pitted black Mission olives
- ½ cup pitted kalamata olives
- 8 anchovy fillets
- ¼ cup balsamic-packed capers, drained
- 5 large garlic cloves
- ⅓ cup extra-virgin olive oil

- 1 round fresh buffalo mozzarella, sliced
- 6 cherry tomatoes, sliced crosswise
- 1½ teaspoons dried thyme
- freshly cracked black pepper
- fresh basil for garnish

classic cherry pies

There really is no time like the present and you shouldn't let another day pass without having tasted one of these cherry pies. They are things of beauty and, as such, will never fade from the annals of my kitchen. This recipe is my Marilyn Monroe, my classic.

INGREDIENTS

Sweet Pâte Brisée (short crust dough)

¾ cup plus 2 tablespoons tapioca flour

¾ cup cornstarch

¼ cup plus 2 tablespoons glutinous rice flour, plus more for dusting

¼ cup sorghum flour

2 tablespoons granulated sugar

¼ teaspoon kosher salt

1½ teaspoons guar gum

1 cup (2 sticks) cold unsalted cultured butter, diced

3 large eggs

Filling

2 cups granulated sugar

¼ cup cornstarch

⅓ cup water

2 pounds fresh Bing cherries, pitted

1¼ teaspoons pure almond extract

¼ teaspoon freshly grated nutmeg

whole milk for brushing

sanding sugar for sprinkling

vanilla ice cream or sweetened whipped cream for serving

MAKES 4 INDIVIDUAL PIES

For the dough: In a stand mixer fitted with the paddle attachment, combine all the dry ingredients and mix on low speed to blend. Add the butter and beat until the mixture resembles coarse bread crumbs. Add the eggs and mix on high speed until the dough turns in on itself. Turn out the dough onto a work surface that has been dusted with rice flour and knead for 3 turns. Divide in half and form each half into a disk. Cover with plastic wrap and refrigerate for at least 2 hours or up to 2 days.

Remove both disks from the refrigerator 15 minutes before rolling out. Dust the work surface again with rice flour and roll out one disk to a 14-inch round. Using an upside-down 4½-inch pie plate as a template, cut out four rounds 1 inch larger than the pan, rerolling the dough as needed.

Fit the pastry rounds into four 4½-inch pie pans.

Roll out the second disk of dough and cut out four more 5-inch rounds. Cut a decorative vent in the center of each round. Place the dough rounds on a baking sheet and refrigerate.

For the filling: In a large, heavy saucepan, combine the granulated sugar and cornstarch and whisk until smooth. Add the water and cherries. Gently stir to coat the cherries, using a very slight pressure so as not to bruise the fruit. Cook, stirring occasionally, over low heat for 20 minutes, or until the juices begin to thicken. If the mixture thickens too much, add more water by tablespoons, stirring after each addition until smooth.

Stir in the almond extract and nutmeg. Remove from the heat and let cool for at least 10 minutes.

Position an oven rack in the center of the oven. Preheat the oven to 425°F. Remove the reserved top crusts from the refrigerator and place beside the prepared pie pans. Fill the pies evenly with the cherry filling.

Brush the edges of a top crust with milk. Center a top crust over a pan and join it to the edge of the bottom crust by pressing the two together. Repeat to top each pie. Brush the top crusts with milk and sprinkle with sanding sugar. Place the pies on a baking sheet and bake for 20 minutes, or until golden brown. Remove from the oven let cool on wire racks.

Serve warm or at room temperature with ice cream or whipped cream.

margarita meringue pie

The name pretty much says it all. I love margaritas and I made this recipe in homage to my favorite cocktail. Made with the juice of Key limes, which are smaller and much more potent than the Persian limes that we are used to here in the States, and infused with a touch of Cointreau and a dash of salt, this pie is the epitome of summer. If Key limes are unavailable in your area, regular limes will work just as well.

MAKES ONE 9-INCH PIE; SERVES 6

Position an oven rack in the center of the oven. Preheat the oven to 400°F.

For the crust: In a medium bowl, combine the graham cracker crumbs, gelatin, cayenne, almond meal, walnuts, and salt. Toss several times with your hands, rolling the ingredients between your fingers to eliminate any large clumps.

Pour the hot butter over the crumb mixture and stir vigorously until it begins to clump. Using your hands, work the mixture to moisten evenly.

Lightly coat a 9-inch glass pie pan with nonstick cooking spray. Pour the crumbs into the pan and then press into place with your hands. Bake for 15 minutes, or until evenly browned. Remove from the oven and let cool completely on a wire rack.

For the filling: If using gelatin sheets, place them in a shallow pan and add just enough water to cover them; let stand for 5 minutes. If using granulated gelatin, put the water in a small bowl, sprinkle the gelatin over, and let stand for 5 minutes.

In a heavy, medium saucepan, heat the condensed milk over medium-low heat until bubbles form around the edges of the pan. Remove from the heat.

If using gelatin sheets, lift the sheets from the water and whisk them into the heated milk. If using granulated gelatin, whisk the gelatin mixture into the hot milk. Stir in the salt, lime zest and juice until smooth and set aside.

In a stand mixer fitted with the whisk attachment, beat the cream until it begins to hold soft peaks. Beat in the sugar and Cointreau just until soft peaks form.

Fold the cream into the lime mixture and then pour into the cooled pie crust. Freeze for 30 minutes and then refrigerate.

For the meringue: In a stand mixer, beat the egg whites on high speed until they are foamy and turn opaque. Add the salt and mix for 30 seconds more on high speed. Add the sugar and cream of tartar and continue to beat on high speed until the meringue forms stiff, glossy peaks.

continued

Graham Cracker Crust

- 1¾ cup gluten-free graham cracker crumbs (about 6 crackers; page 75)
- 1 envelope unflavored gelatin
- ⅛ teaspoon cayenne pepper
- 2 tablespoons almond meal
- 2 tablespoons finely chopped walnuts
- pinch of kosher salt
- ½ cup (1 stick) unsalted butter, melted and hot
- nonstick cooking spray

Filling

- 4 gelatin sheets, or 1 envelope plus 1 teaspoon unflavored granulated gelatin
- ⅓ cup water for granulated gelatin
- one 14-ounce can sweetened condensed milk
- ⅛ teaspoon kosher salt
- 2 tablespoons lime zest
- 1 cup fresh Key lime juice
- 1¼ cups heavy cream
- 2 tablespoons sugar
- 2 tablespoons Cointreau liqueur

Meringue

- 6 large egg whites
- ⅛ teaspoon kosher salt
- ½ cup confectioners' sugar
- ¼ teaspoon cream of tartar

margarita meringue pie, continued

Remove the pie from the refrigerator and pile the meringue on top of the filling. Make sure the meringue is spread all the way to the edges of the crust to prevent shrinkage. Using a kitchen torch, brown the top of the meringue. Alternatively, brown the pie under a preheated broiler at least 6 inches from the heat source for about 45 seconds. Take care, as the meringue can burn quickly. Cut into wedges to serve.

Store in the refrigerator for up to 1 day.

BLACKBIRD BAKING TIP

Meringue pies are best the day they are made. The sugar in the meringue will absorb moisture from the filling and the air, causing the egg whites to dissolve. The liquid they release is known as "weeping."

deep-dish apple pie

My most coveted pie is of the apple variety. To me, nothing says an afternoon out by the grill better than having an apple pie to finish off the experience. What sets this pie apart from your normal apple pie is that I use a whopping thirteen apples that I slowly cook down with Vietnamese cinnamon and brown sugar, creating a collection of flavors so distinctively comforting, you'll never search for another apple pie recipe. Use Maker's Mark bourbon as it is currently the only gluten-free bourbon available.

MAKES ONE 12-INCH DEEP-DISH PIE; SERVES 8 TO 10

Peel, core, and thinly slice all the apples and put in a very large bowl. Pour the lemon juice over the apples and toss. In a small bowl, combine the granulated sugar, light brown sugar, dark brown sugar, cornstarch, cinnamon, nutmeg, and salt and toss with a fork until there are no longer any lumps. Pour the dry ingredients over the apples, toss, and let stand for 5 minutes.

In a large Dutch oven, melt the butter and then add the apple mixture. Stir to coat the apples in the butter and cook down for 10 minutes. Add the bourbon and ½ cup of the water and cook over medium heat, stirring frequently, for 20 minutes, or until the apples are tender and the sugar has caramelized. If the mixture begins to thicken too much, add the remaining ½ cup water, reduce the heat to low, and continue to cook, stirring occasionally to prevent sticking, about 15 minutes longer.

Remove both disks of dough from the refrigerator and let stand for 15 minutes. Position an oven rack in the center of the oven. Preheat the oven to 400°F.

Dust the work surface with glutinous rice flour and roll one of the dough disks out to a 14-inch round.

Gingerly transfer the rolled dough to a 12-inch deep-dish pie pan, fitting the dough into the pan and being cautious not to tear the dough, as it is delicate. (If you do tear the dough, just join the tear together and brush the tear with water; smooth with your finger until the damage is no longer visible.) Using scissors, trim the overhanging dough to an even 1 inch.

continued

INGREDIENTS

Filling

13 mixed baking apples: Golden Delicious, Braeburn, or Red Delicious and either Gala or Fuji

juice of 1 large lemon

1 cup granulated sugar

½ cup packed light brown sugar

⅓ cup dark brown sugar

4 tablespoons cornstarch

2 teaspoons ground cinnamon

¼ teaspoon grated nutmeg

¼ teaspoon kosher salt

3 tablespoons cold unsalted butter, diced

2 tablespoons Maker's Mark bourbon

1 scant cup of water

2 disks Sweet Pâte Brisée (short crust dough; page 98)

glutinous rice flour for dusting

milk for brushing

sanding sugar for sprinkling

vanilla ice cream for serving

deep-dish apple pie, continued

Roll out the second disk of dough to a 14-inch round, adding additional rice flour, if needed. Trim the edges. Using decorative cookie cutters, press into the center of the disk to form a vent. Set aside.

Pour the filling into the pie shell. Brush the overhang of the bottom crust with water. Fold the pie top in half, center the vent hole and unfold. Pinch the top layer of dough to the bottom and then flute the edges with your fingers.

Brush the dough with milk and sprinkle with sanding sugar. Bake for 30 to 40 minutes, or until golden brown.

Remove from the oven and let cool on a wire rack for at least 2 hours before slicing. Serve cut into wedges and topped with vanilla ice cream.

Cover and store for up to 2 days at room temperature or refrigerate for up to 1 week.

blueberry cobbler

INGREDIENTS

Filling

¼ cup cornstarch

1 cup granulated sugar

¾ teaspoon ground cinnamon

juice of 1 lemon, strained

4 cups fresh or frozen
   blueberries

butter for the pan

Topping

½ cup sorghum flour

½ cup cornstarch

⅓ cup tapioca flour

2 tablespoons corn flour

1 teaspoon guar gum

2 teaspoons baking powder

¼ teaspoon baking soda

½ teaspoon kosher salt

½ cup (1 stick) cold unsalted
   butter, diced

⅔ cup organic buttermilk

sanding sugar for sprinkling

vanilla ice cream for serving

Blueberry cobbler has been one of my favorite desserts since I was a tadpole. The tang of the buttermilk biscuits combined with the explosively sweet warm blueberries and the cool wash of vanilla ice cream is a lesson in edible joy. Here's a gluten-free version that will blow off the top of your head with pleasure.

MAKES ONE 8-INCH SQUARE COBBLER; SERVES 8 TO 10

For the filling: In a large, heavy saucepan, combine the cornstarch, granulated sugar, and cinnamon. Stir with a fork until there are no lumps and the cornstarch is evenly incorporated. Stir in the lemon juice and half of the blueberries, taking care not to smash the berries. Cook over medium heat until the blueberries begin to bubble, about 5 minutes. Carefully stir in the remaining blueberries and turn off the heat.

Position an oven rack in the center of the oven. Preheat the oven to 425°F. Butter an 8-inch square baking pan and set it on a baking sheet. Pour the filling into the pan.

For the topping: In a medium bowl, combine all the dry ingredients and stir with a whisk to blend. Add the butter and, using a pastry cutter, cut it in until the mixture resembles coarse bread crumbs. Add the buttermilk and stir until all the dry ingredients are moistened. Using an ice-cream scoop, arrange mounds of dough on top of the blueberries. Sprinkle with the sanding sugar and bake for 20 minutes, or until golden. Remove from the oven and let cool for 30 minutes on a wire rack. Serve warm, with vanilla ice cream.

Store, lightly covered, at room temperature for 24 hours or up to 3 days in the refrigerator.

cakes, big & small

individual almond-raspberry cakes

¾ cup Almond Paste (page 112)

½ cup (1 stick) unsalted butter at room temperature

¼ cup sugar

3 tablespoons sorghum flour

2 tablespoons tapioca flour

pinch of kosher salt

1⅛ teaspoons baking powder

1 teaspoon guar gum

3 large eggs

1¼ teaspoons almond extract

1½ cups raspberry preserves, such as Bonne Maman, heated and then strained

I went through this phase where my obsession with almonds and their myriad possibilities had me baking with them daily for months. I was dumbfounded by their versatility and delicate nature. How could one food be so endlessly changeable and yet so enduringly delicious? These cakes are made with homemade almond paste, as store-bought almond paste is not gluten-free.

MAKES 8 INDIVIDUAL CAKES

Position an oven rack in the center of the oven. Preheat the oven to 350°F. Butter a 9-by-13-inch pan. Line the pan with sheets of parchment paper, being careful to cover both the bottom and the sides; leave ½-inch excess parchment on two of the sides. Butter the parchment paper.

In a stand mixer fitted with the paddle attachment, combine the almond paste, butter, and sugar and beat on low speed until blended. Increase the speed to medium-high and beat until thick and smooth.

In a small bowl, combine all the dry ingredients and stir with a small whisk to blend. Add to the butter mixture and beat on medium-low speed until blended, stopping to scrape down the sides of the bowl once or twice.

Turn the mixer on low speed and add the eggs, one at a time, then the almond extract. Increase the speed to high and beat for 1 minute, or until light and fluffy.

Pour the batter into the prepared pan and smooth the top. Bake for 30 to 35 minutes, or until golden brown. Rotate the pan after 15 to 20 minutes of baking to insure even browning.

Remove from the oven and let cool completely in the pan on a wire rack. Remove the cake from the pan by lifting the edges the of parchment paper. Transfer to a cutting board. Using a 2½-inch biscuit cutter, cut out eight rounds. Cut each round in thirds horizontally. Spread one round with raspberry preserves and top with the second round. Spread the second round with more preserves. Top with the remaining round. Repeat to make a total of eight cakes. Ice the top of the cakes with the remaining raspberry preserves.

almond paste

1¼ cups almond meal

1¼ cups confectioners' sugar, sifted, plus more for dusting

⅓ cup water

3 tablespoons plus 1 teaspoon granulated sugar

1 tablespoon plus 1 teaspoon light corn syrup

In a food processor, mix the almond meal and 1¼ cups confectioners' sugar and pulse to combine.

In a small, heavy saucepan, add the water, granulated sugar, and corn syrup. Cook over medium heat, stirring to dissolve the sugar, and bring just to a boil. Add to the almond meal mixture and pulse several times, then beat on high speed for several seconds to make a very soft, sticky paste.

Lightly dust the almond paste with additional confectioners' sugar. Knead several times.

Store in an airtight container in a cool, dark place for up to 1 year.

suisses

I love to travel, not only because it allows me to see life from a whole new perspective, but because of the food I encounter along the way. I discovered these very traditional petits fours while cooking in the Franche-Comté region of France in the Jura, which shares a border with Switzerland. During a day trip to Besancon, I saw these little *gateaux de cerises au kirsch,* or "cherry cakes with kirsch," as I passed a bakery and desperately wanted to try them, but never could. So when I returned home I vowed to eradicate that little problem; the payoff was well worth the wait.

MAKES 40 PETITS FOURS

For the genoise: Position an oven rack in the center of the oven. Preheat the oven to 350°F. Butter a jellyroll pan and line it with parchment paper. Butter the paper.

In a small bowl, combine all the dry ingredients and stir with a small whisk to blend. Pour the butter over the dry ingredients. Whisk until smooth and set aside.

In a stand mixer fitted with the whisk attachment, beat together the eggs, sugar, and almond extract until the mixture is thick enough to leave a slowly dissolving ribbon on the surface when the whisk is lifted.

Stir the butter mixture into the egg mixture until smooth. Pour the batter into the prepared pan, smooth the top, and bake for 15 to 20 minutes, or until the sides pull slightly away from the sides of the pan and the cake is set and springy when touched.

Remove from the oven and let cool completely in the pan on a wire rack.

For the strawberry buttercream: In a small, heavy saucepan, cook the sugar and water over medium-low heat until the temperature registers 239°F (soft-ball stage) on a candy thermometer.

Meanwhile, using a stand mixer fitted with the whisk attachment, beat the egg yolks just until blended. With the machine running on medium speed, add the hot sugar mixture, then beat on maximum speed until the mixture is cool and increases four times in volume to form a thick mousse, 4 to 5 minutes. Cream the butter in a separate bowl and gradually add it to the cool egg yolk mixture and beat until very smooth.

In a blender, puree the strawberries, then force them through a fine-mesh sieve into a bowl with the back of a large spoon. Add the puree and kirsch to the buttercream and beat until smooth. Fit a pastry bag with a ½-inch plain tip and fill it with the buttercream.

continued

INGREDIENTS

Genoise

- 6 tablespoons sorghum flour
- 6 tablespoons cornstarch
- ¼ cup tapioca flour
- 2 teaspoons baking powder
- 1 tablespoon guar gum
- 1 cup (2 sticks) unsalted butter, melted
- 8 large eggs
- 1 cup plus 2 tablespoons sugar
- 1 tablespoon almond extract

Strawberry Buttercream

- 1 cup sugar
- ½ cup water
- 6 large egg yolks
- 1¼ cups (2½ sticks) unsalted butter at room temperature
- 1½ cups fresh strawberries
- 2 tablespoons kirsch liqueur

- 20 candied (glacé) cherries, halved

Quick Fondant

- 1 cup sugar
- ½ cup water
- 1½ tablespoons light corn syrup
- 1 teaspoon kirsch
- 2 cups powdered sugar

Using a 1¾-inch round cookie cutter, cut 40 rounds from the genoise. Pipe a generous mound of buttercream on top of each cake round and then top each petit four with a halved candied cherry. Refrigerate while you make the fondant.

For the fondant: In a small, heavy saucepan, combine the granulated sugar, water, and corn syrup. Cook over medium heat, tilting the pan back and forth several times to keep the sugar from settling, until the mixture registers 239°F (soft-ball stage) on a candy thermometer. Remove from the heat. In a stand mixer fitted with a paddle attachment, pour in the powdered sugar and the hot syrup. Beat on medium-high speed for 1 to 2 minutes, until the mixture begins to thicken. Add the kirsch and mix until smooth. If the icing is too thick, add a few more drops of kirsch.

Place the cakes on wire racks set in jellyroll pans and pour the icing over each cake until evenly coated. You should be able to see the cherry through the icing. Let stand 15 minutes before serving.

ABOUT PETITS FOURS

So what exactly is a petit four? The name, in French, literally means "little oven." According to Carême, the famous nineteenth-century French chef, the name comes from the fact that these little cakes were originally baked in a low wood-fired oven, after the big cakes had come out and the temperature of the oven had gone down. Today, the beautiful iced wee cakes are usually made with genoise, layered with myriad fillings, and iced with fondant.

chestnut genoise hearts

These individual heart-shaped cakes have a robust chestnut flavor, a delicate buttercream filling, and a perfectly sweet glaze, resulting in a subtly complex dessert that will make even the hardest of hearts swoon.

MAKES 4 HEARTS

For the genoise: Position an oven rack in the center of the oven. Preheat the oven to 350°F. Butter a jellyroll pan, line the pan with parchment paper, and butter the paper. In a small bowl, combine all the dry ingredients and stir with a small whisk to blend.

In a stand mixer fitted with the whisk attachment, beat the eggs until they begin to froth. Add the granulated sugar and vanilla and beat on high speed for about 5 minutes, or until the mixture is doubled in volume and forms a slowly dissolving ribbon on the surface when the whisk is lifted.

Fold the dry ingredients into the egg mixture, then stir in the butter just until blended.

Pour the batter into the prepared pan and smooth the top. Bake for 15 to 20 minutes, or until the cake pulls slightly away from the sides of the pan and is set and springy when touched. Remove from the oven and let cool completely in the pan on a wire rack.

Meanwhile, for the buttercream: In a small, heavy saucepan, combine the sugar and water. Bring to a boil over medium heat and cook until the temperature registers 239°F (soft-ball stage) on a candy thermometer.

Meanwhile, using a stand mixer fitted with the whisk attachment, beat the egg yolks until blended. When the sugar reaches the soft-ball stage, immediately pour it into the egg yolks and beat on high speed until thick and mousse-like. Beat in the vanilla just to combine.

In a separate bowl, whisk the butter until light and smooth. Gradually fold in to the cooled egg yolk mixture until smooth. Using a firm spatula, transfer the buttercream to a pastry bag fitted with a ⅝-inch plain tip and set aside.

For the glaçage: In a medium saucepan, combine the confectioners' sugar, water, and maple syrup. Whisk until smooth. Turn the heat on low and whisk in the maple butter until smooth. Remove from the heat and pour into a glass bowl and let cool to the touch, stirring often to prevent a skin from forming.

Using a 3-inch heart-shaped cookie cutter, cut eight hearts from the genoise. Place the hearts on a wire rack set over a jellyroll pan. Carefully pipe the buttercream on four of the hearts and then top each heart with another layer of genoise. Flood the tops of each cake with glaçage until the entire cake has a uniform coating. Let stand for 30 minutes to set the glaze.

These may be stored in the refrigerator for up to 3 days.

INGREDIENTS

Genoise

- 6 tablespoons chestnut flour
- ¼ cup cornstarch
- 6 tablespoons tapioca flour
- 2 teaspoons baking powder
- 1 tablespoon guar gum
- 8 large eggs
- 1 cup plus 2 tablespoons granulated sugar
- 2½ teaspoons pure vanilla extract
- 1 cup (2 sticks) unsalted butter, preferably cultured, melted

Buttercream

- ¾ cup granulated sugar
- 6 tablespoons water
- 4 large egg yolks
- 1½ teaspoons pure vanilla extract
- 1 cup (2 sticks) unsalted butter at room temperature

Glaçage

- 2 cups confectioners' sugar, sifted
- 3 tablespoons water
- ¼ cup grade A dark amber maple syrup
- 1 teaspoon maple butter

cream cheese shortcakes with macerated cherries

This delectable summertime treat is a refreshing close to any meal served under the stars. The sweetness comes from the fresh cherries rather than the shortcakes. Flashes of tart and sweet will dance on your tongue as the cicadas play their rhythmic song, while everything slows down to that familiar summertime purr as the fireflies rise up from the freshly cut grass like miniature stars, begging to be caught.

SERVES 6

In a medium bowl, combine the cherries and sugar. Toss until all of the cherries are evenly coated. Cover and refrigerate for at least 1 hour or up to 3 hours.

Meanwhile, for the shortcakes: Position an oven rack in the center of the oven. Preheat the oven to 425°F. Butter a 9-inch cake pan and line with a round of parchment paper. Butter the paper.

In a large bowl, combine all the dry ingredients, including the sugar. Using a pastry cutter, cut in the cream cheese and butter into the dry ingredients until the mixture resembles coarse bread crumbs. Drizzle the buttermilk and vanilla and almond extract over the dough and stir in just until incorporated.

Dust a work surface with tapioca flour. Turn out the dough onto the surface and coat with tapioca flour to prevent the dough from sticking to your hands. Quickly shape the dough into a 9-inch round. Using a 2-inch round cookie cutter, cut out six shortcakes. Arrange the cakes in the prepared pan and bake for 15 minutes, or until lightly browned. Remove from the oven and place the pan on a wire rack.

For the kirsch-infused cream: Using a stand mixer fitted with the whisk attachment, beat the cream until it thickens lightly. Add the sugar and kirsch and beat until soft peaks form.

Cut a shortcake in half and top the bottom piece with a nice layer of whipped cream. Place a large spoonful of cherries on the cream and then balance the top half of the shortcake on the cherries. Repeat to make 6 desserts.

For best results, serve the shortcakes the same day they are prepared. If you wish to serve the shortcakes warm, place them in a preheated 300°F oven for 3 minutes.

young-coconut cupcakes

1⅓ cups plus 1 tablespoon sorghum flour

⅔ cup plus 1 tablespoon cornstarch

⅔ cup plus 1 tablespoon tapioca flour

2 cups granulated sugar

1 tablespoon guar gum

1 tablespoon baking powder

¾ teaspoon kosher salt

1 cup (2 sticks) unsalted butter, room temperature, diced

5 large eggs, beaten

1 cup organic buttermilk

¼ cup fresh young-coconut juice

1 tablespoon pure vanilla extract

2 tablespoons pure almond extract

one 16-ounce package sweetened shredded coconut

Cream Cheese Frosting (page 122)

½ cup sliced almonds, toasted (see note), for garnish

Fresh young-coconut juice, the naturally occurring clear liquid found inside a coconut before it has matured, is one of the most gorgeous flavors on the planet. Nutty base notes reign supreme above the unmistakable coconut flavor and just get my taste buds all in a tizzy. These rich cupcakes are proof of my devotion.

Fresh young-coconut juice may be found at your local juice bar or at natural foods stores such as Whole Foods.

MAKES 24 LARGE CUPCAKES OR 48 MINI CUPCAKES

Position an oven rack in the center of the oven. Preheat the oven to 350°F. Line 24 standard muffin cups or 48 miniature muffin cups with paper liners.

In a stand mixer fitted with the paddle attachment, combine all the dry ingredients and mix on low to blend. Add the butter and beat on low speed until the lumps of butter are no longer visible.

Add the eggs and beat for 30 seconds. Add the buttermilk, coconut juice, and vanilla and almond extract and gradually increase the speed to high, one gear at a time, to prevent splashing. Mix for 1½ minutes, or until smooth. Scrape down the bowl as necessary. Fold in the coconut.

Using an ice-cream scoop or a spoon, fill each prepared cup three-fourths full with batter. Bake 12 to 15 minutes for mini cakes and 20 minutes for standard ones, or until the cakes are golden and set. Remove from the oven, let cool for a few minutes and then unmold onto wire racks. Turn the cupcakes right-side up so the tops don't get indentations from the rack. Let cool completely.

Using an offset spatula, ice the top of each cupcake with a generous dollop of icing. Garnish with the toasted almonds.

Store in an airtight container for up to 2 days.

toasting sliced almonds

Preheat the oven to 350°F. Spread the almonds in a pie pan and toast for about 5 minutes, or until fragrant and lightly golden. Immediately remove from the oven and pour the almonds into a bowl to stop the cooking process.

cream cheese frosting

½ cup (1 stick) unsalted butter, preferably cultured, at room temperature

two 8-ounce packages cream cheese at room temperature

2 cups confectioners' sugar

1½ teaspoons pure vanilla extract

In a stand mixer fitted with the paddle attachment, cream the butter on medium speed until very smooth. Scrape down the sides of the bowl and add the cream cheese. Beat on medium-high speed until smooth. Sift the confectioners' sugar over the cream cheese mixture and beat again until satiny. Beat in the vanilla just until combined. Use now, or cover and refrigerate for up to 1 week. If storing in the fridge, allow the icing to soften and stir thoroughly before using.

dark chocolate–peanut butter cupcakes

I love these cupcakes not just for their moist crumb, but also for their icing. After one try, you'll see what I mean. They're like peanut butter cups on steroids.

MAKES 12 CUPCAKES

Position an oven rack in the center of the oven. Preheat the oven to 350°F. Line 12 muffin cups with paper liners and set aside.

In a stand mixer fitted with the paddle attachment, combine all the dry ingredients and mix on low speed to blend. Add the butter and beat until blended. Increase the speed to medium and add the egg, buttermilk, and vanilla. Beat on high speed until smooth. Using an ice-cream scoop, fill each muffin cup three-fourths full with batter. Bake for 20 to 25 minutes, or until springy to the touch.

Remove from the oven and unmold onto wire racks. Turn right-side up and let cool completely.

Using an offset spatula, frost the cooled cupcakes.

These are best served the day they're baked, but they may be stored in an airtight container for up to 2 days.

INGREDIENTS

- 1 cup granulated sugar
- ½ cup unsweetened Dutch-processed cocoa powder
- ½ cup millet flour
- ¼ cup tapioca flour
- ¼ cup cornstarch
- 5 tablespoons glutinous rice flour
- ⅛ teaspoon baking powder
- ½ teaspoon baking soda
- ¼ teaspoon salt
- ½ cup (1 stick) plus 2 tablespoons unsalted butter at room temperature
- 1 large egg
- ¾ cup organic buttermilk
- 2 teaspoons pure vanilla extract
- Peanut Butter Icing (page 124)

peanut butter icing

MAKES 2 CUPS

6 tablespoons unsalted butter at room temperature

¼ cup packed light brown sugar

2 tablespoons dark brown sugar

¼ teaspoon kosher salt

1 cup creamy peanut butter

1 cup confectioners' sugar, sifted

¼ cup heavy cream

1 teaspoon pure vanilla extract

In a stand mixer fitted with the paddle attachment, cream the butter with the light and dark brown sugars and the salt until it forms a ball. Add the peanut butter and mix until smooth, stopping to scrape down the sides of the bowl once or twice. Beat in the confectioner's sugar, cream, and vanilla. Beat on medium speed until light and fluffy, about 45 seconds. Do not overwhip the icing, as it will cause the butter to melt.

cactus caramel cupcakes

INGREDIENTS

⅔ cup sorghum flour

⅓ cup cornstarch

⅓ cup tapioca flour

2 teaspoons guar gum

1½ teaspoons baking powder

heaping ¼ teaspoon kosher salt

1 cup granulated sugar

6 tablespoons unsalted butter, preferably cultured, diced

3 large eggs

¼ cup sour cream

1 tablespoon pure vanilla extract

½ cup organic buttermilk

Caramel Icing (page 128)

½ cup green sugar for decorating, or color of your choice

Adorable to behold and divine to devour, these little cupcakes have a tendency to make any baker feel accomplished. It's the satiny caramel icing that looks so impressive (well, it is one of the oldest American recipes, dating to 1880; also known as burnt sugar icing, it's a Southern classic). I decorated mine with a green-sugar cactus, because that was the original design I used for my son Leo's birthday a few years back, but you can use any design you want.

MAKES 12 CUPCAKES

Position an oven rack in the center of the oven. Preheat the oven to 350°F. Line 12 muffin cups with paper liners.

In a large stand mixer fitted with the paddle attachment, combine all the dry ingredients and mix on low speed to blend. Add the butter and mix until the dough begins to come away from the sides of the bowl.

In a medium bowl, whisk together the eggs and sour cream until very smooth. Add the vanilla and whisk until blended. Alternating the egg mixture with the buttermilk, add the wet ingredients to the dry ones in two increments. Beat on high speed until light and fluffy.

Fill the prepared muffin cups three-fourths full with batter and bake for 15 minutes, or until the tops of the cupcakes are just barely colored and springy to the touch.

Remove from the oven and let cool for 5 minutes in the pan. Unmold the cupcakes onto wire racks and turn them right-side up to cool completely.

Using an offset spatula, ice the cupcakes, making the icing as smooth as possible. Using a cactus cookie cutter or another shape, place the cutter in the center of an iced cupcake. Apply gentle pressure to create a seal between the icing and the cookie cutter. Using a demitasse spoon, carefully fill the cookie cutter with sugar sprinkles. Tap the side of the cupcake to ensure the icing is evenly coated and the motif is clear. Holding on to the cutter, invert the cupcake to eliminate any excess sugar. Turn the cupcake right-side up and gently remove the cookie cutter. Repeat this process until all of your cupcakes are decorated.

These are best the day they are baked, but they may be stored in an airtight container for up to 2 days.

caramel icing

1½ cups confectioners' sugar, sifted

1   teaspoon pure vanilla extract

¼ cup (½ stick) plus 1 tablespoon unsalted butter

1¼ cups packed light brown sugar

2   tablespoons light corn syrup

pinch of kosher salt

¼ cup heavy cream

1   to 3 tablespoons water, if needed

In a stand mixer fitted with the paddle attachment, combine the confectioners' sugar and vanilla. In heavy medium saucepan, combine the butter, brown sugar, corn syrup, and salt. Bring to a boil over medium heat. Remove from the heat and immediately whisk in the heavy cream. Whisk for 1 minute. Add to the sugar and vanilla in the mixer bowl and mix on high speed until very smooth. Pour the mixture into a clean glass bowl. The icing should move very slowly when you tilt the bowl from side to side. If the icing seems too thick, beat in water, 1 teaspoon at a time, until you have achieved the right consistency.

chocolate-chocolate icing

8 ounces semisweet chocolate chips

1½ cups (3 sticks) unsalted butter at room temperature

1⅓ cups confectioners' sugar

1 cup unsweetened cocoa powder

1 cup light corn syrup

1½ teaspoons pure vanilla extract

In a double boiler over barely simmering water, melt the chocolate chips. Stir to smooth. Remove from the heat and let cool to room temperature.

In a food processor, pulse the butter just until smooth. Combine the remaining icing ingredients and pulse several times until silken. Do not overmix, as this will cause the butter to melt. Add the cooled melted chocolate and pulse several times more until blended. Transfer to a glass bowl and stir several times with a rubber spatula.

chocolate cake, squared

This cake is devilishly good and appropriate for any chocolate-lover, as it is made with chocolate in four different forms. The moist crumb of the cake and the richness of the icing make this a very noble birthday cake.

MAKES ONE 8-INCH FOUR-LAYER CAKE; SERVES 8

Position an oven rack in the center of the oven. Preheat the oven to 350°F. Butter two 8-inch round cake pans. Line each pan with a round of parchment paper and butter the paper.

In a stand mixer fitted with the paddle attachment, combine all the dry ingredients and mix on low speed to blend. Add the butter and continue to mix on low speed until blended.

Add the eggs, safflower oil, milk, and vanilla. Beat on medium-high speed until smooth.

Evenly divide the batter between the two pans and smooth the tops. Rotating the pans after 15 minutes, bake for 30 minutes, or until the cakes begin to pull away from the sides of the pans and a toothpick inserted into the center comes out clean.

Remove from the oven and let cool in the pans on wire racks for 5 minutes. Run a butter knife around the edges of the pans and unmold the cakes onto wire racks to cool completely. Remove the parchment paper and turn the cake rounds right-side up.

Using a very sharp serrated knife, level the top of both cake rounds if necessary. Cut each cake round in half horizontally to make four rounds. Place a cake round on a wire rack set on a jellyroll pan and generously brush with the chocolate liqueur. This will de-crumb the cake and add a lovely flavor dimension.

Choose a cake stand or serving plate and drop a dollop of icing in the center of the platter to secure the bottom layer of the cake. Position the liqueur-brushed cake layer over the icing and press down gently. Spread ¼ cup of the icing over the top of the cake layer. Place a second layer on the wire rack and brush with the liqueur, then place this layer on top of the first one. Repeat brushing and filling until all the layers have been used. Ice the top and sides of the cake with a very thin layer of icing and then refrigerate to set it, about 15 minutes. Remove the cake from the refrigerator and pile the remaining icing on top. Using an offset spatula, frost the top and sides evenly. Let the cake stand in a cool place for about 1 hour before slicing. Cut into wedges to serve.

Store in a cool place for up to 3 days.

INGREDIENTS

- ¼ cup sorghum flour
- ½ cup cornstarch
- ½ cup millet flour
- 1 cup glutinous rice flour
- ½ cup tapioca flour
- 2½ teaspoons baking powder
- ½ teaspoon guar gum
- ½ teaspoon kosher salt
- ⅔ cup unsweetened Dutch-processed cocoa powder
- 1⅓ cups granulated sugar
- 1 cup (2 sticks) unsalted butter at room temperature, diced
- 4 large eggs
- ½ cup safflower oil
- 1 cup whole milk
- 3 tablespoons pure vanilla extract
- ½ cup chocolate liqueur, such as Godiva, for brushing the cake

Chocolate-Chocolate Icing (page 129)

angelle's german chocolate cake

- ½ cup boiling water
- 4 ounces bittersweet chocolate, chopped
- 1 cup tapioca flour
- ¾ cup sorghum flour
- ½ cup cornstarch
- 2 teaspoons baking powder
- 2 teaspoons guar gum
- ½ teaspoon kosher salt
- 1¾ cups sugar
- 1 cup (2 sticks) unsalted butter at room temperature
- 4 large eggs
- 1 cup organic buttermilk
- 1 tablespoon pure vanilla extract
- Pecan-Coconut Frosting (page 136)

My good friend Angelle requested that I devise a gluten-free version of her favorite birthday cake, German chocolate, to see if it could match the wheat-flour versions she'd come to love so dearly over the years. The cake was so well received I promised the recipe would be named after her.

MAKES ONE 9-INCH THREE-LAYER CAKE; SERVES 12

Preheat the oven to 350°F. Butter three 8-inch round cake pans and line the bottom of each with a round of parchment paper. Butter the paper.

Pour the boiling water over the chocolate in a small bowl. Let stand for 3 minutes, then whisk until smooth. Set aside and let cool.

In a medium bowl, combine all the dry ingredients and stir with a whisk to blend.

In a stand mixer fitted with the paddle attachment, cream the butter until very smooth. Add the dry ingredients and mix on low speed until smooth, stopping once or twice to scrape down the sides of the bowl.

Add the eggs and mix on medium-high speed for 1 minute. Add the buttermilk and vanilla and mix on high speed for 1 minute, or until light and fluffy.

Reduce the mixer speed to low and gradually pour in the melted chocolate. Beat until blended, stopping once or twice to scrape down the sides of the bowl. Divide the batter among the prepared pans. Gently shake each to release any bubbles and to even the level of the batter.

Bake for 25 minutes, or until the cakes have pulled away from the sides of the pans. Rotate the pans from back to front and from one rack to another after 15 minutes of baking.

Remove from the oven and let cool for 10 minutes in the pans on wire racks. Run a knife around the edge of each pan and unmold onto a wire rack. Remove the parchment paper and turn the cake rounds right-side up. Let cool completely.

Frost the top of one cake round with ½ cup of the frosting. Repeat with the second round. Using an offset spatula, carefully ice the top of the cake. Cut into wedges to serve.

Store in a covered cake keeper at room temperature for 2 days or up to 1 week in the refrigerator.

the hummingbird cake

I had never heard of a hummingbird cake until my friend and neighbor Mark Meyer requested that I make one for his birthday. It was so delicious I had to pinch myself. It was like eating banana bread with a side of pineapple. This cake is wonderful with cream cheese icing and stellar with seven-minute icing; you can decide for yourself. This cake originated in Jamaica, where the hummingbird, also called the "doctor bird," is a national symbol; the cake is known there as the doctor bird cake. This cake isn't traditionally made with coconut; I added it as a decidedly delectable option.

MAKES ONE 8-INCH LAYER CAKE

Position an oven rack in the center of the oven. Preheat the oven to 350°F. Butter two 8-inch cake pans. Line each pan with a round of parchment paper and butter the paper.

In a large bowl, combine all the dry ingredients, including the sugar and spices. Stir with a whisk to blend. Spread the pecans in a pie pan and bake for 10 minutes, or until fragrant. Pour into a bowl and let cool for 5 minutes. Using a large knife, chop the pecans.

Mash the bananas in a large bowl. Add the pineapple, agave nectar, and vanilla. Stir until smooth.

Add the safflower oil and eggs to the dry ingredients and stir until smooth. Add the toasted pecans and the pineapple mixture and stir until blended. Fold in coconut (if using).

Divide the batter between the two prepared pans and smooth the tops. Cover each pan with aluminum foil and bake for 50 minutes. Uncover and bake for 10 minutes more.

Remove from the oven and let cool completely in the pans on wire racks.

Frost with the cream cheese or seven-minute icing. Spread ½ cup frosting over one layer for a filling, then top with the second layer. If using the cream cheese frosting, cover the top and sides of the cake with a crumb coat (a very thin layer of frosting) and refrigerate for 10 minutes to set it (this keeps crumbs out of the final coat of frosting). Finish the cake by frosting the top and sides, making swirls in the cream cheese frosting and little peaks in the seven-minute icing.

INGREDIENTS

- ½ cup cornstarch
- ½ cup millet flour
- ½ cup glutinous rice flour
- ¼ cup tapioca flour
- ½ cup almond meal
- ½ cup sorghum flour
- 2 teaspoons baking powder
- 1½ teaspoons guar gum
- 1½ teaspoons kosher salt
- 2 cups sugar
- 1 teaspoon ground cinnamon
- ½ teaspoon freshly grated nutmeg
- 1 cup pecans
- 2 very ripe bananas
- 1 cup canned crushed pineapple (in juice, not syrup)
- ¼ cup agave nectar
- 1 tablespoon pure vanilla extract
- 1 cup safflower oil
- 3 large eggs, beaten
- 1 cup shredded coconut (optional)
- 1 double recipe Cream Cheese Frosting (page 122) or Seven-Minute Icing (page 137)

pecan-coconut frosting

MAKES 4½ CUPS

12 egg yolks

3 cups sugar

3 cups heavy cream

3 sticks (1½ cups) unsalted butter

6 cups shredded sweetened coconut

3½ cups chopped Texas pecans

    In a heavy-bottomed saucepan, whisk the egg yolks, sugar, and cream together until smooth. Add the butter and cook over medium heat, stirring constantly until the mixture comes to a boil. Remove from the heat and fold in the coconut and pecans. Pour into a large bowl and let cool completely. The icing continues to thicken as it cools.

seven-minute icing

MAKES ENOUGH TO FILL AND FROST
ONE 8-INCH TWO-LAYER CAKE

1½ cups sugar

¾ cup water

6 large egg whites

¼ teaspoon kosher salt

¼ teaspoon plus ⅛ teaspoon cream of tartar

1½ teaspoons pure vanilla extract

In a small, heavy saucepan, combine the sugar and the water. Bring to a boil over medium-high heat, whisking to dissolve the sugar, and cook until the mixture registers 239°F (soft-ball stage) on a candy thermometer. This will take several minutes.

Meanwhile, in a stand mixer fitted with the whisk attachment, beat the egg whites with the salt until frothy and opaque. Add the cream of tartar, and continue to beat on high until thick and foamy. Add the vanilla and beat to blend.

When the sugar mixture has reached the correct temperature, immediately pour the hot sugar into the egg whites with the mixer on high speed and beat for 5 to 7 minutes, or until stiff, glossy peaks form.

pineapple upside-down cake

I grew up on this magnificent pineapple upside-down cake, and some of my fondest memories are of my mother inverting the cake, unveiling the caramelized and glistening fruit, bathed in a wash of syrup and pure buttery beauty.

MAKES ONE 8-INCH CAKE; SERVES 6

Position an oven rack in the center of the oven. Preheat the oven to 350°F. Lightly coat an 8-inch round cake pan with nonstick cooking spray.

For the topping: In a 12-inch skillet, combine the water, light and dark brown sugars, and vanilla bean. Bring to a gentle boil over medium-high heat and cook, stirring until the sugar is completely dissolved. Reduce the heat to medium-low, add the pineapple slices, and sauté each side for about 3 to 5 minutes, or until lightly browned. Using a slotted metal spatula, carefully transfer the slices to a plate and let cool. Cook the sugar mixture in the pan to reduce to about ⅓ cup. Remove from the heat and stir in the butter and coconut rum. Remove the vanilla bean and set the syrup aside.

For the batter: In a stand mixer fitted with the paddle attachment, combine all the dry ingredients and mix on low speed to blend. Add the butter and mix on low speed until blended. Add the eggs and beat on medium-high speed for 1 minute, or until light and fluffy. With the machine running, gradually add the buttermilk and beat until blended, stopping to scrape down the sides of the bowl once or twice. Add the vanilla and beat for 1 minute more. Set aside.

Arrange four of the pineapple slices in the bottom of the prepared pan. Cut the remaining slices in half to make half-moons and arrange them around the edges of the pan, curved-side up, gently pressing the slices so they stick to the sides. Place a maraschino cherry in the center of each of the four pineapple slices lining the bottom of the pan. Cut the remaining cherries in half. Place one half in the arch of the half slices, being careful to have the cut side of the cherries facing the inside of the pan. Pour the sugar syrup over the pineapple slices lining the bottom of the pan. Quickly pour the batter over the pineapples and cherries. Smooth the surface with an offset spatula. Bake for 45 to 55 minutes, or until the cake is lightly browned and a toothpick inserted in the center comes out clean.

Remove from the oven and let cool for 2 to 3 minutes. Gently run a knife around the edge of the pan. Unmold onto a serving plate and let cool for 15 minutes before slicing. Cut into wedges and serve warm or at room temperature, with vanilla ice cream.

Store, lightly covered, on the counter for up to 2 days or refrigerate for up to 1 week.

INGREDIENTS

nonstick cooking spray

Topping

- 1 cup water
- ¾ cup packed light brown sugar
- ¼ cup packed dark brown sugar
- 1 vanilla bean, split lengthwise
- 1 ripe pineapple, peeled, cut into ten ¼-inch-thick crosswise slices, and cored
- 1 tablespoon unsalted butter
- 2 tablespoons coconut rum

Batter

- 1 cup granulated sugar
- ½ cup sorghum flour
- ¼ cup glutinous rice flour
- ¼ cup cornstarch flour
- ½ cup tapioca flour
- ½ teaspoon baking soda
- ¾ teaspoon baking powder
- ¼ teaspoon kosher salt
- 7 tablespoons unsalted butter at room temperature
- 2 large eggs
- ¾ cup organic buttermilk
- 1½ teaspoons pure vanilla extract

10 maraschino cherries

vanilla ice cream for serving

coconut tres leches

INGREDIENTS

- 1 cup white rice flour
- 1 cup sorghum flour
- ¼ cup tapioca flour
- 1 teaspoon kosher salt
- 2 teaspoons baking powder
- ¼ teaspoon freshly grated nutmeg
- 4 tablespoons unsalted butter at room temperature
- ¼ cup canola oil
- 1½ cups sugar
- 7 large egg yolks
- 1 cup unsweetened coconut milk
- 1 teaspoon coconut extract
- 5 large egg whites

Tres Leches Syrup

- 1 cup heavy cream
- one 14-ounce can sweetened condensed milk
- one 12-ounce can evaporated milk

Coconut Seven-Minute Icing (page 142)

When dining out for Mexican food in the South, you almost always find a tres leches, or "three milks," cake on the dessert menu for one reason: It is absolutely scrumptious. Nothing can compare with its three layers of cream, unfolding in your mouth in successive soft waves. The gorgeous thing about this cake is that the colder it gets, the better it tastes, so you can make it well in advance to really let the flavors marry while saving time for other preparations. For my take on this Mexican classic, I added coconut, making a classic even classier.

MAKES ONE 8-INCH CAKE; SERVES 10

Position an oven rack in the center of the oven. Preheat the oven to 350°F. Lightly butter an 8-inch square baking pan and set aside.

In a medium bowl, combine all the dry ingredients and stir with a whisk to blend. In a stand mixer fitted with the paddle attachment, combine the butter, oil, and sugar. Beat on medium-high speed until the sugar is evenly moistened, about 45 seconds. Add the egg yolks and beat on high until smooth. On low speed, add the dry ingredients and beat until blended. Increase the speed to high and beat for 2 minutes more, or until thick and smooth. Add the coconut milk and coconut extract and beat until smooth. Add the egg whites and beat on high speed for 3 minutes.

Pour the batter into the prepared pan, smooth the top, and cover with aluminum foil to prevent over-browning. Bake for 50 minutes to 1 hour, or until the cake is golden and a toothpick inserted in the center comes out clean.

Just before the cake is ready to come out of the oven, make the syrup: In a medium bowl, whisk together the cream, condensed milk, and evaporated milk until smooth.

Remove the cake from the oven and let cool for a few minutes. Using a long wooden skewer, poke a couple dozen holes in the cake. Immediately pour the tres leches syrup over the cake. Cover with aluminum foil and refrigerate overnight.

Remove the cake from the refrigerator and ice the cake. Return to the refrigerator until ready to serve. Cut into squares to serve.

Store, lightly covered, in the refrigerator for up to 1 week.

coconut seven-minute icing

½ cup sugar

¼ cup water

2 large egg whites

pinch of kosher salt

⅛ teaspoon cream of tartar

½ teaspoon pure vanilla extract

1 cup sweetened shredded coconut

    In a small, heavy saucepan, combine the sugar and water. Bring to a
boil over medium-high heat, tilting the pan back and forth several times
to make sure the sugar has dissolved, and cook until the temperature
registers 239°F (soft-ball stage) on a candy thermometer. This will take
several minutes.

    Meanwhile, in a stand mixer fitted with the whisk attachment, combine
the egg whites and salt. Beat until opaque and frothy. Add the cream of
tartar and continue to beat on high speed until thick and foamy. Beat in the
vanilla until blended.

    When the sugar mixture reaches 239°F, immediately pour it into the
egg whites with the mixer on high speed and beat for 5 to 7 minutes, or
until the egg whites form stiff, glossy peaks. Remove the whisk and the
bowl from the mixer and fold in the coconut.

new york–style cheesecake with amaretti crust

This baby is big, like the city it's named for, and it's almost as busy, with a multitude of fabulous, bright flavors. A traditional New York–style cheesecake is one that has a graham-cracker crust and a batter made with just eggs, sugar, cream cheese, and sour cream or heavy cream. This recipe uses both heavy cream and sour cream, and the crust is made with ground almonds and amaretti cookies. This version will surprise you, no matter where you live.

MAKES ONE 9-INCH CAKE; SERVES 10

Position an oven rack in the center of the oven. Preheat the oven to 325°F. Butter a 9-inch springform pan.

For the crust: In a food processor, pulse the sliced almonds and amaretti until finely ground. Add the guar gum and pulse a few more times. Pour the crumbs into a bowl.

In a stand mixer fitted with the paddle attachment, beat together the butter and sugar on medium speed for 3 minutes, or until light and fluffy. Add the crumb mixture and beat on medium speed until the mixture resembles small peas.

Scoop the mixture out of the bowl and sprinkle evenly in the prepared pan. Press firmly on the mixture to evenly cover the bottom. The crust should come about a half inch up the sides of the pan. Bake for 12 minutes, or until golden brown. Remove from the oven and let cool completely on a wire rack. Increase the oven temperature to 500°F.

Meanwhile, for the filling: In a stand mixer fitted with the paddle attachment, combine the cream cheese and sugar. Beat on medium-high speed for 3 minutes. Stop to scrape down the sides of the bowl and mix for 3 minutes more, or until silky smooth. (This is crucial for eliminating any lumps in the mixture.) Scrape down the bowl again and add the sour cream, heavy cream, and salt. Beat on medium speed until smooth. Scrape down the bowl again and add the eggs, one at a time, mixing for a full minute after each addition. Add the vanilla with the fourth egg and beat for 2 minutes on medium-high speed.

continued

INGREDIENTS

Crust

1 cup sliced almonds

7 double-wrapped Lazzaroni amaretti cookies (14 cookies total)

3½ tablespoons guar gum

5 tablespoons unsalted butter at room temperature

2½ tablespoons sugar

Filling

four 8-ounce packages cream cheese at room temperature

1⅓ cups sugar

1 cup sour cream

⅓ cup heavy cream

½ teaspoon kosher salt

4 large eggs at room temperature

2 teaspoons pure vanilla extract

new york–style cheesecake
with amaretti crust, continued

Pour the filling into the cake pan and set the cake pan on a baking sheet. Bake at 500°F for 10 minutes, then immediately reduce the oven temperature to 200°F and bake for 1 hour and 40 minutes, or until the top of the cake is golden and the center is set. Transfer the cake to a wire rack and let cool for 15 minutes. Run a knife around the edges of the pan so that when the cake begins to contract, it will not tear. Let cool for about 2 hours, then cover with plastic wrap and refrigerate overnight.

The next day, remove the plastic wrap and the sides of the pan. Dip a very sharp knife into hot water and cut the cake into wedges, dipping the knife before and after each cut, wiping off the blade as necessary.

Store in the refrigerator, tightly covered, for up to 3 days.

CHAPTER FIVE

crepes & pâte à choux

savory crepes

Crepes are so versatile that I decided they had to be included in this book. They really do act as a springboard for creativity. Use your own imagination to vary the filling, but whatever you do, don't skip the vodka in the batter. It is *the* ingredient that makes the batter light enough to create that trademark lace-like edge.

MAKES 8 TO 10 CREPES

INGREDIENTS

¼ cup sorghum flour

¼ cup tapioca flour

¼ cup cornstarch

2 tablespoons glutinous rice flour

1 teaspoon guar gum

½ teaspoon kosher salt

1¼ cups chicken stock

4 tablespoons unsalted butter, melted

3 large eggs, beaten

1 tablespoon vodka

¼ cup water

4 tablespoons clarified unsalted butter (page 15) for the pan

In a blender or food processor, combine all the dry ingredients with ½ cup of the chicken stock and blend. With the blender on medium speed, drizzle in the melted butter followed by the remaining ¾ cup chicken stock; blend for 30 seconds. Add the eggs and blend until incorporated. Blend in the vodka and water, then cover and refrigerate for at least 30 minutes or up to 1 hour.

Remove the batter from the refrigerator. It should be the consistency of heavy cream. If the batter seems too thick, whisk in more stock or water a tablespoon at a time until the right consistency.

In a 10-inch crepe pan or skillet, heat 1 teaspoon of the clarified butter over high heat and swirl the butter to coat the pan evenly.

Pour a generous ¼ cup batter into the pan and tilt the pan to coat the bottom evenly. Cook until browned on the bottom, about 1½ minutes, then turn and cook on the second side until browned, about 1 minute. Transfer to a plate. Repeat to use the remaining batter, adding clarified butter as needed, stacking the finished crepes as you go.

To store, tightly cover the crepes with plastic wrap and refrigerate for up to 3 days.

crepes suisses

SERVES 4

Lay 2 crepes on a baking sheet and top with 1 slice gluten-free ham and 2 tablespoons shredded Swiss cheese. Fold in half. Repeat to make 8 filled crepes. Place the crepes on a baking sheet and bake in a preheated 400°F oven for 3 minutes. Garnish with minced fresh parsley and chives.

mushroom crepes with cream

Another variation using the savory crepes that will become a mainstay—use the best mushrooms you can find. Other mushroom varieties, such as baby 'bellas, oyster, and maiitake, can be substituted in this filling.

SERVES 4

In a heavy, medium saucepan, melt 2 tablespoons of the butter over medium heat and sauté the shallots for 3 minutes, or until translucent. Add the remaining 4 tablespoons butter and heat until melted. Add the mushrooms and season with salt and pepper. Sauté for 7 to 10 minutes, or until the mushrooms have released their liquid and look uniformly wilted. Add the cream and cook until it boils. Remove from the heat and stir in the 2 teaspoons parsley. The sauce should be thick, not runny.

Spoon about ¼ cup of the mushroom mixture in a line down the center of a crepe and fold over two opposite sides. Repeat to fill the remaining crepes.

Serve 2 filled crepes per person, garnished with parsley.

INGREDIENTS

- 6 tablespoons unsalted butter
- ¼ cup diced shallots
- 2 ounces shiitake mushrooms, stemmed and thinly sliced
- 2 ounces cremini mushrooms, thinly sliced
- 2 ounces alba clamshell mushrooms, trimmed
- 1¼ teaspoons kosher salt
- freshly ground pepper
- 1 cup heavy cream
- 2 teaspoons minced fresh flat-leaf parsley, plus more for garnish
- 8 Savory Crepes (page 149)

sweet crepes

Here is a master recipe for sweet crepes, with two variations. Be sure to include the spirits in these recipes as it gives the batter just the right consistency. Create your own favorite versions by varying the spirits (think rum, Cognac, Grand Marnier, or other liqueurs) and the fillings.

MAKES 8 CREPES

In a blender or food processor, combine all the dry ingredients with ½ cup of the milk and blend. With the blender on medium speed, drizzle in the melted butter, followed by the remaining ¾ cup milk; blend for 30 seconds. Add the eggs and blend until incorporated. Blend in the Cointreau and water, then cover and refrigerate for at least 30 minutes or up to 1 hour.

Remove the batter from the refrigerator. It should be the consistency of heavy cream. If the batter seems too thick, whisk in more water 1 tablespoon at a time until the right consistency.

In a 10-inch crepe pan or skillet, heat 1 teaspoon of the clarified butter over high heat and swirl the butter to coat the pan evenly.

Pour a generous ¼ cup batter into the pan and tilt the pan to coat the bottom evenly. Cook until browned on the bottom, about 1½ minutes, then turn and cook on the second side until browned, about 1 minute. Transfer to a plate. Repeat to use the remaining batter, adding clarified butter as needed, stacking the finished crepes as you go.

The crepes may be tightly covered in plastic wrap and refrigerated for up to 3 days.

nutella triangles
SERVES 4

Make the batter for the sweet crepes, substituting 1 tablespoon Frangelica liqueur for the Cointreau. Spread 1 tablespoon Nutella on a crepe. Fold in half, then fold again to make a triangle. Repeat to make 8 crepes.

cinnamon sugar cigarettes
SERVES 4

Make the batter for the sweet crepes, using 1 tablespoon brandy or Cognac in place of the Cointreau. Combine ⅓ cup sugar and 1 teaspoon ground cinnamon. Brush each crepe with melted butter and sprinkle with the cinnamon sugar. Roll the crepes like cigarettes and serve.

INGREDIENTS

- ¼ cup sorghum flour
- 5 tablespoons tapioca flour
- ¼ cup cornstarch
- 1 teaspoon guar gum
- ½ teaspoon kosher salt
- 1¼ cups whole milk
- 4 tablespoons unsalted butter, melted
- 3 large eggs, beaten
- 1 tablespoon Cointreau liqueur
- ¼ cup water
- 4 tablespoons clarified unsalted butter (page 15) for the pan

mandarin orange crepes

Mandarin oranges and Cointreau-flavored cream cheese combine to make sweet-tart crepes that are bright with color and flavor.

INGREDIENTS

- one 8-ounce package cream cheese at room temperature
- ¼ cup confectioners' sugar, sifted
- ¼ teaspoon vanilla extract
- 1½ teaspoons orange zest, preferably mandarin
- ½ cup strained fresh orange juice
- ¼ cup granulated sugar
- 2 tablespoons Cointreau liqueur
- 32 canned mandarin orange wedges
- 8 Sweet Crepes (page 153)

SERVES 4

In a stand mixer fitted with the paddle attachment, beat the cream cheese until very smooth. Add the confectioners' sugar, vanilla, and zest, beating on high speed until smooth, about 1 minute, stopping to scrape down the sides of the bowl at least once.

In a small, heavy saucepan, combine the orange juice and granulated sugar. Bring to a boil over medium-high heat and cook to reduce until syrupy. Stir in the Cointreau and set aside.

Spoon about 3 tablespoons filling in a line down the center of a crepe, leaving a border. Fold the crepe like an envelope. Place, folded-side down, on a dessert plate. Repeat to fill the remaining crepes, with 2 per serving. Place 4 of the mandarin orange wedges on top of each filled crepe and spoon some of the syrup over the orange wedges.

Serve immediately.

blintzes

I grew up on blintzes and my brothers and sisters and I loved them so much we would elbow each other to get the latest ones off the griddle. There was nothing more comforting than waking up to the smell of these small wonders frying in the pan, and the coffee roasting in the pot, and the sound of my mom clinking bowls and clanging spoons to make it all happen.

MAKES 8 BLINTZES; SERVES 4

For the batter: In a small bowl, combine all the dry ingredients. Stir with a small whisk to blend.

In a stand mixer fitted with the whisk attachment, beat the eggs until blended. With the machine running, alternately add the dry ingredients with the milk in three batches, beating until smooth. Beat in the water and melted butter until blended. The batter should be the consistency of heavy cream. If the batter is too thick, add milk 1 tablespoon at a time until the consistency is right.

For the filling: In a large bowl, combine all the ingredients and stir vigorously to blend.

In a 10-inch skillet, melt the ½ tablespoon butter over medium-high heat until it foams. Pour a generous ¼ cup of batter into the pan and quickly tilt the pan to coat the bottom evenly. Cook until the edges begin to crinkle and pull away from the pan, about 1 minute. Flip the blintz and cook for 30 seconds. Spoon 2 tablespoons filling into the center of the crepe and fold in the sides. Transfer to a plate and keep warm in a low oven while cooking and filling the remaining blitzes. Immediately serve 2 blintzes per person, with preserves of choice.

INGREDIENTS

Batter

¼ cup cornstarch

¼ cup sorghum flour

¼ cup tapioca flour

2 teaspoons guar gum

½ teaspoon kosher salt

3 large eggs

1 cup whole milk, plus more if needed

4 tablespoons unsalted butter, melted and cooled

¼ cup water

Filling

16 ounces cottage cheese

¼ cup sugar

¼ teaspoon ground cinnamon

1½ teaspoons pure vanilla extract

½ tablespoon unsalted butter

fruit preserves of choice for serving

choux au fromage

Pâte à choux, the base for these puffs of air with a hint of Gruyère cheese, is an extremely versatile pastry that is both beautiful and effusively light, two qualities that are difficult to achieve in baking. In fact, choux paste is so malleable, it can be piped into any shape, including swans for a dramatic take on profiteroles, and it is delicious whether served sweet or savory. So you can imagine my pride when I mastered a gluten-free version of this culinary giant.

Choux au fromage are an excellent way to begin a meal and are sublime when filled with chicken salad and served as an hors d'oeuvre.

INGREDIENTS

2 tablespoons sorghum flour

2 tablespoons tapioca flour

¼ cup glutinous rice flour

¼ cup cornstarch

1 teaspoon guar gum

5 tablespoons unsalted butter

5 tablespoons water

5 tablespoons half-and-half

1½ tablespoons sugar

¼ teaspoon kosher salt

½ cup shredded Gruyère cheese

3 large eggs

1 large egg white

1 teaspoon baking powder

MAKES ABOUT 12 CHEESE PUFFS

Position an oven rack in the center of the oven. Preheat the oven to 425°F. Line a baking sheet with parchment paper or a silicone baking mat.

In a small bowl, combine the flours, cornstarch, and guar gum and stir with a small whisk to combine.

In a heavy, medium saucepan, combine the butter, water, half-and-half, sugar, and salt. Cook over medium-low heat until the butter has melted and the mixture comes to a gentle boil. Add the dry ingredients and stir vigorously, using a scraping motion, for 3 minutes, or until the dough pulls away from the sides of the pan and leaves a thin film on the bottom of the pan.

Immediately transfer the dough to a food processor, add the cheese, and pulse for 20 seconds to cool slightly. In a small bowl, whisk the eggs and egg white until blended. Add the baking powder and whisk until smooth. With the machine running, gradually add the egg mixture to the food processor and process to make a thick, sticky paste, about 1½ minutes.

Fit a pastry bag with a 1-inch plain tip and fill the bag with the choux paste. Pipe mounds of paste, each about 1½ inches in diameter, 2 inches apart on the prepared pan. You should have 12 mounds. Using the back of a wet teaspoon, smooth the tops of the cheese puffs and then bake for 15 minutes. Do not open the oven door during this time. Reduce the oven temperature to 375°F and bake for 7 minutes more, or until the puffs are golden brown.

Remove from the oven and pierce the side of each puff with a paring knife. Return to the turned-off oven with the door ajar for 10 minutes. Transfer to a wire rack and let cool slightly or completely. Serve warm or at room temperature.

Will keep in an airtight container for 1 day.

cream puffs

I love cream and custards more than I can say, and when you add cream puffs as the vehicle to deliver these heavenly delights, well, that pretty much seals the deal. If you've never served cream puffs at a brunch, I highly recommend it, as they go beautifully with mimosas.

MAKES 12 LARGE CREAM PUFFS

Position an oven rack in the center of the oven. Preheat the oven to 425°F. Line a baking sheet with parchment paper or a silicone baking mat.

For the Pâte à Choux: In a small bowl, combine the sorghum and tapioca flours, cornstarch, and guar gum. Stir with a small whisk to blend.

In a heavy, medium saucepan, combine the butter, water, half-and-half, granulated sugar, and salt. Cook over medium-low heat until the butter has melted and the mixture comes to a gentle boil.

Add the dry ingredients and stir vigorously with a wooden spoon, using a scraping motion, for 3 minutes, or until the dough pulls away from the sides of the pan and leaves a film on the bottom of the pan.

Immediately transfer the dough to a food processor and pulse for 20 seconds to cool slightly. In a small bowl, whisk together the eggs and egg white, then whisk in the baking powder. With the food processor running, gradually add the egg mixture to make a thick, sticky paste, about 1½ minutes.

Fit a pastry bag with a 1-inch plain tip and fill the bag with the Pâte à Choux. Pipe mounds of paste, each about 1½ inches wide, 2 inches apart on the prepared pan. You should have 12 mounds. Using the back of a wet teaspoon, smooth the tops of the cream puffs and bake for 15 minutes. Do not open the oven door during this time. Reduce the oven temperature to 375°F and bake for 7 minutes more, or until the puffs are golden brown.

Remove the puffs from the oven and pierce the side of each one with a paring knife. Return to the turned-off oven with the door ajar for 10 minutes. Transfer to wire racks to cool completely.

Cut the cooled cream puffs in half crosswise. Transfer the pastry cream to a pastry bag fitted with a small plain tip. Fill the bottom half of each cream puff with pastry cream and top with the other half. Repeat until all the puffs are filled with cream. Dust with confectioners' sugar and serve.

These are best served the day they are baked, but may be stored for 1 day in an airtight container.

INGREDIENTS

Pâte à Choux

- 1 tablespoon sorghum flour
- 2 tablespoons tapioca flour
- 5 tablespoons cornstarch
- 1 teaspoon guar gum
- 5 tablespoons unsalted butter
- 5 tablespoons water
- 2 tablespoons half-and-half
- ½ teapoon granulated sugar
- ¼ teaspoon kosher salt
- 2 large eggs
- 1 large egg white
- ¾ teaspoon baking powder
- 1 recipe Pastry Cream (page 162)

confectioners' sugar for dusting

éclairs

1 recipe Pâte à Choux
 (page 161)

Pastry Cream

2 cups whole milk

2 teaspoons pure vanilla
 extract

3 tablespoons cornstarch

½ cup plus 2 tablespoons
 granulated sugar

6 large egg yolks

⅛ teaspoon kosher salt

Chocolate Glaze

3 ounces bittersweet
 chocolate, chopped

1½ tablespoons unsalted butter

1½ tablespoons water

1 tablespoon light corn syrup

¼ cup sugar

I always joke that éclairs are the French equivalent of a doughnut, and these are an incredible take on that notion. I like to really fill each choux with pastry cream so it explodes when you bite into it.

MAKES ABOUT 7 ÉCLAIRS

Position an oven rack in the center of the oven. Preheat the oven to 425°F. Line a baking sheet with parchment paper or a silicone mat.

Fit a pastry bag with a 1-inch plain tip and fill the bag with the choux paste. Pipe 2-inch-long ribbons of paste 2 inches apart on the prepared pan. You should have 7. Using the back of a wet teaspoon, smooth the tops of the choux and bake for 15 minutes. Do not open the oven door during this time. Reduce the oven temperature to 375°F and bake for 7 minutes more, or until golden brown. Remove from the oven and pierce the side of each éclair with a paring knife. Return to the turned-off oven with the door ajar for 10 minutes. Transfer to wire racks to cool completely.

For the pastry cream: In a medium, heavy saucepan, combine the milk and vanilla. Cook over medium heat until bubbles form around the edges of the pan. Meanwhile, combine the cornstarch, sugar, and egg yolks in a medium bowl and whisk until the mixture forms a slowly dissolving ribbon on the surface when the whisk is lifted.

Gradually whisk the hot milk into the eggs. Return to the pan and cook over medium-low heat, stirring constantly with a wooden spoon, until the mixture begins to thicken. Stir in the salt and cook until the spoon leaves a trail in the cream. Remove from the heat, pour into a medium bowl, and let cool completely.

For the glaze: In a double boiler over simmering water, melt the butter and chocolate. Stir to make sure the mixture is super smooth. Add the remaining ingredients, stir, and remove from the heat and let cool. The glaze should be smooth but not runny.

Fit a pastry bag with a small plain tip, and fill the bag with the pastry cream. Pierce the end of an éclair with the pastry tip and fill it with the pastry cream. Repeat to fill the remaining éclairs.

Using a frosting spatula, ice the tops of the éclairs. Let the glaze set for 10 minutes before serving.

Serve within 4 hours of filling the éclairs.

profiteroles

After I mastered the pâte à choux recipe, I made profiteroles every chance I had. After about the seventh time I served them, however, my family looked at me with this expression that clearly revealed that they were wondering if I had a disease of the brain. When I finally asked what was wrong, the reply I got was, "Really? Again?"

MAKES ABOUT 20 PROFITEROLES; SERVES 10

Position an oven rack in the center of the oven. Preheat the oven to 425°F. Line a baking sheet with parchment paper or a silicone mat.

Fit a pastry bag with a 1-inch plain tip and fill the bag with the choux paste. Pipe 2-inch-diameter mounds of paste 1½ inches apart on the prepared pan. You should have 20. Using the back of a wet teaspoon, smooth the tops of the mounds and bake for 15 minutes; do not open the oven during this time. Reduce the oven temperature to 375°F and bake for 7 minutes, or until golden brown.

Remove from the oven and pierce the side of each puff with a paring knife. Return to the turned-off oven with the door ajar for 10 minutes. Transfer to wire racks to cool completely.

For the sauce: In a small, heavy saucepan, combine the half-and-half, sugar, and corn syrup and cook until the mixture comes to a soft boil. Remove from the heat and add the chocolate. Let sit for 3 minutes, then whisk until smooth. Whisk in the Calvados, water, and salt until smooth. If the sauce appears too thick, whisk in additional water, 1 tablespoon at a time.

Cut each puff in half and fill each half with a generous scoop of vanilla ice cream, then place the top half of the puff on top of the ice cream. Place 2 puffs on each dessert plate and pour the chocolate sauce over the puffs. Garnish with mint sprigs, if desired.

Fill and serve these the day they are made. The unfilled puffs may be stored in an airtight container for 1 day.

INGREDIENTS

1 recipe Pâte à Choux (page 161)

Rich Chocolate Sauce

⅔ cup plus 3 tablespoons half-and-half

3 tablespoons sugar

3 tablespoons plus 1 teaspoon light corn syrup

8 ounces bittersweet chocolate, chopped

2 teaspoons fine Calvados brandy

3 tablespoons water

pinch of salt

vanilla ice cream for serving

mint sprigs for garnish (optional)

CHAPTER SIX

custards, puddings & ice cream

basil-infused custard with lemon chantilly cream

What could be more refreshing than two of the brightest flavors of summer brought together in the form of a custard? I wholeheartedly recommend that you use free-range organic eggs when you make this or any custard, as the yolks in these eggs are similar to the farm eggs I found in France. Farm eggs have deep orange yolks, giving custards both color and flavor.

INGREDIENTS

2½ cups whole milk

1½ cups sugar

40 fresh basil leaves (from about 4 sprigs), plus more leaves for garnish

¼ cup cornstarch

1 large egg

6 large egg yolks

Lemon Chantilly Cream

1 cup heavy cream

2½ tablespoons sugar

¼ teaspoon pure vanilla extract

1 teaspoon grated lemon zest

SERVES 7

In a large, heavy saucepan, combine the milk, ½ cup of the sugar, and the 40 basil leaves. Cook over medium heat until bubbles form around the edges of the pan. Remove from the heat and let stand for 15 minutes.

Meanwhile, in a medium bowl, combine the cornstarch and the remaining 1 cup sugar. Stir with a whisk to blend. Add the egg and egg yolks and whisk vigorously until pale in color.

Strain the milk mixture into a bowl. Temper the eggs by gradually whisking the warm milk into the them. Return to the pan and cook over low heat, stirring constantly, until the mixture begins to thicken, about 15 minutes. Whisk for about 7 minutes, until smooth.

Remove from the heat and divide the custard among seven 6-ounce custard cups. Refrigerate for at least 4 hours or, preferably, overnight.

For the Chantilly cream: In a stand mixer fitted with the whisk attachment, beat the cream on high speed until it holds soft folds. Add the sugar, vanilla, and lemon zest and beat until soft peaks are formed.

To serve, top each custard with a dollop of lemon cream and garnish with a basil sprig.

BLACKBIRD BAKING TIP

This custard is delicious as a tart filling as well.

white truffle honey–infused panna cottas

This recipe was inspired by a cheese plate I once had while dining in Rome. The assorted cheeses were served with a crystallized white truffle honey. I nearly fell over from the intense combination of sensory pleasure and my childlike fascination with the clever pairing. Here, I've infused acacia honey with white truffle oil to achieve this same flavor in a creamy panna cotta, but clover honey will work if you can't get your hands on the acacia variety.

SERVES 8

Note: You will need to infuse the honey at least 12 hours before using.

Lightly oil eight 4-ounce ramekins. If using gelatin sheets, place them in a shallow pan and add water to cover; let stand for 15 minutes. If using granulated gelatin, sprinkle it over 2 tablespoons water.

In a heavy, medium saucepan, combine the cream, milk, sugar, and infused honey. Cook over low heat until bubbles form around the edges of the pan. Do not allow to come to a boil. Immediately remove from the heat and transfer to a bowl. If using gelatin sheets, squeeze the excess water from them and whisk into the hot cream until smooth. If using granulated gelatin, whisk until smooth.

Stir in the crème fraîche just until smooth (overmixing will cause air bubbles to form). Evenly divide the mixture among the prepared ramekins. Let cool, then refrigerate for at least 4 hours or up to 2 days.

To serve: Drizzle each plate with the balsamic. Dip the bottom of each ramekin in a warm-water bath for a few seconds, then invert the ramekin onto the plate. Garnish each panna cotta with a halved fig.

white truffle–infused honey

MAKES ⅓ CUP

In a glass jar, combine 1 teaspoon white truffle oil and ⅓ cup acacia honey. Stir until the honey is opaque. Cover with a tight-fitting lid and infuse in a cool, dark place for at least 12 hours or up to 6 months.

INGREDIENTS

- 3 gelatin sheets, or 1 envelope unflavored granulated gelatin
- 2 cups heavy cream
- 1 cup whole milk
- ¾ cup sugar
- 2 tablespoons White Truffle-Infused Honey (recipe follows)
- 1 cup crème fraîche
- 4 fresh black Mission figs, stemmed and halved
- 25-year-old balsamic vinegar for drizzling

ginger crème brûlée

INGREDIENTS

2 cups heavy cream

1 cup sliced peeled fresh ginger

⅓ cup plus 6 tablespoons sugar

6 large egg yolks

mint sprigs and julienned candied ginger for garnish

Custards became my quiet meditation while I was cooking in France. They became a balm after the days of struggling with foreign language and ingredients, treks to the market, and the nonstop meticulous prepping of food. When I just wanted something to work without question, I always made a custard to make myself feel better.

After all of my experiments of infusing with the various herbs I found growing in and around the château, custards became not only my source of calm, but a medium for creativity, revealing the limitless potential of this lovely dessert.

MAKES 6 CUSTARDS

Position an oven rack in the center of the oven. Preheat the oven to 400°F.

In a small, heavy saucepan, combine the cream and ginger and cook over low heat until bubbles form around the edges of the pan. Remove from the heat and let stand for 15 minutes. Meanwhile, in a medium bowl, combine the ⅓ cup sugar and the egg yolks. Whisk until the mixture thickens and forms a slowly dissolving ribbon on the surface when the whisk is lifted.

Set six 4-ounce ramekins or custard cups in a roasting pan. Strain the scalded cream into another bowl and discard the ginger slices. Gradually whisk the cream into the egg yolk mixture. Strain the mixture through a fine-mesh sieve and evenly divide among the ramekins. Add cold water to the roasting pan to come halfway up the sides of the ramekins.

Bake for 12 to 15 minutes, or until the custards are set on the edges and the centers tremble when gently rocked back and forth. The custards will set fully as they are chilled.

Remove from the oven and let cool. Refrigerate for at least 4 hours or up to 5 days. Sprinkle 1 tablespoon sugar evenly over each custard. Place under a preheated broiler, at least 4 inches from the heat source, for about 45 seconds, or until the sugar has caramelized. You can also use a kitchen torch to achieve the same effect.

Remove from the oven and let cool. Serve garnished with mint sprigs and julienned candied ginger.

triple-chocolate mint parfaits

With chocolate pudding, mellow mint-chocolate mousse, and dark chocolate custard, this parfait will have you waxing poetic after the first bite. Each layer is infused with a varying chocolatiness, creating such a complex tableaux of flavors, you'll find yourself licking the spoon in an effort to savor them all.

MAKES 6 LARGE PARFAITS

For the chocolate pudding: In the top of a double boiler, combine the cornstarch, sugar, and salt. Whisk well until there are no longer any lumps. Pour the milk into the dry ingredients and whisk well. Cook over medium heat, stirring occasionally, until thick and smooth, 12 to 15 minutes. Remove from the heat and add the semi-sweet chocolate and vanilla. Whisk until silky smooth. Strain through a fine-mesh sieve and set aside.

For the chocolate mousse: In a small, medium saucepan, combine the milk and mint leaves. Cook over low heat just until the mixture comes to a low boil. Remove from the heat and infuse for 15 minutes.

Place the bittersweet chocolate in a bowl and strain the milk into the bowl. Let stand for 5 minutes. Whisk until smooth. Let the chocolate cool to the touch, about 10 minutes. Whisk in the egg yolks and set aside.

In a deep bowl, beat the cream until soft peaks form. Fold into the melted chocolate. Beat the egg whites with the sugar until stiff, glossy peaks form. Fold into the chocolate mixture just until blended. Set aside.

For the chocolate custard: In a heavy, medium pan, heat the cream over medium-low heat just until it comes to a boil. Put the chocolate in a bowl and pour the hot cream over. Let stand for 5 minutes, then whisk until smooth.

In a small bowl, whisk together the egg yolks and sugar until a slowly dissolving ribbon forms on the surface when the whisk is lifted. Gradually whisk in the chocolate mixture until smooth. Return to the pan and cook, stirring constantly, over medium-low heat until the mixture coats the back of a spoon. Remove from the heat. Press a sheet of plastic wrap directly on the surface of the custard and set aside.

In each of six 8-ounce cylindrical glasses, pour ⅓ cup dark chocolate custard; ⅓ chocolate pudding; then ⅓ cup mint chocolate mousse. Cover and refrigerate for at least 2 hours or overnight. To serve, top with whipped cream and garnish with mint sprigs.

INGREDIENTS

Chocolate Pudding

¼ cup cornstarch

⅔ cup sugar

⅛ teaspoon kosher salt

3 cups whole milk

6 ounces semisweet chocolate, finely chopped

2 teaspoons pure vanilla extract

Rich Mint Chocolate Mousse

⅓ cup whole milk

20 fresh mint leaves

4 ounces bittersweet chocolate, finely chopped

2 large eggs, separated

½ cup heavy cream

¼ cup sugar

Dark Chocolate Custard

2 cups heavy cream

6 ounces unsweetened chocolate, finely chopped

4 large egg yolks

¼ cup sugar

sweetened whipped cream for serving

mint sprigs for garnish

rice pudding *(arroz con leche)*

The aromatic jasmine rice in this Spanish rice pudding is the key to creating a deep, rich flavor that cannot be imitated. I cook this pudding very slowly over low heat so the raisins become engorged with cream, causing this seemingly simple dessert to become operatic.

INGREDIENTS

1   cup jasmine rice

3   cups water

2   cinnamon sticks

¼   teaspoon kosher salt

1½ cups sugar

3   large eggs, beaten

4   cups whole milk

1   cup raisins

1½ teaspoons pure vanilla
    extract

ground cinnamon for dusting

SERVES 6

In a large, heavy saucepan, combine the rice, water, cinnamon sticks, and salt. Bring to a boil over medium heat, stir once to ensure that no rice is sticking to the pan, and then reduce the heat to low. Cover with a tight-fitting lid and cook until almost all of the water has been absorbed, about 15 minutes. Remove from the heat and set aside, covered. Remove the cinnamon sticks.

While the rice is cooking, whisk ½ cup of the sugar into the eggs. In a medium, heavy saucepan, combine the milk and the remaining 1 cup sugar. Cook over low heat, stirring a couple of times to fully dissolve the sugar, until bubbles begin to form around the edges of the pan. Gradually whisk half of the hot milk into the egg mixture. Add this mixture to the remaining hot milk in the pan and stir until combined. Add the raisins and let stand for 10 minutes.

Uncover the rice and gradually stir in the custard. Place over very low heat and cook, stirring frequently, until very thick, about 30 to 40 minutes. Do not let boil, or the eggs will curdle. Remove from the heat and stir in the vanilla. Let stand for at least 2 hours before serving, or cover and refrigerate overnight.

To serve, spoon into bowls or parfait glasses and dust with cinnamon.

The pudding may be covered and stored in the refrigerator for up to 4 days.

cheeky peach ice cream

In the gloaming of summer days, after the sun had set below the horizon, my mother would call out for us to meet in the backyard to help turn the crank on our ice-cream maker. Invariably, I would still be in my bathing suit from the morning swim, and the bottoms of my bare feet would be black from running through the day. My mom would descend the stairs with a canister filled with Fredericksburg peaches and fresh cream and nestle it into the ice-cream maker. Without complaint, my brothers and sisters and I would willingly take turns cranking the machine in the near dark until it would no longer turn and the top of the canister bulged with the fruits of our labor.

For the very best results, use the most fragrant peaches you can get your hands on. In Texas, the peaches that come from Fredericksburg, a little town an hour and a half outside of Austin, are legendary.

MAKES 2 QUARTS

In a heavy, medium pan, heat the half-and-half over medium-low heat until bubbles form around the edges of the pan.

Meanwhile, in a medium bowl, whisk together the eggs, egg yolks, the 6 tablespoons granulated sugar, the brown sugar, and salt until silky smooth. Gradually whisk half of the hot half-and-half into the egg mixture. Return to the pan and cook over medium heat, stirring constantly, until the custard begins to thicken, about 5 minutes. Remove from the heat, pour into a large bowl, and stir in the vanilla and almond extract. Let cool and refrigerate for at least 2 hours or overnight. Pour the ¾ cup sugar over the chopped peaches in a large bowl, toss lightly, and let stand until the sugar has completely dissolved.

If you have a 2-quart ice-cream maker, pour all the chilled custard into it; if your ice-cream maker holds only 1 quart, you'll need to freeze the custard in two batches. Add the heavy cream (or ½ cup cream for a 1-quart machine) and freeze according to the manufacturer's instructions until thick but not completely frozen. Then add the peaches (or half of them, if using a 1-quart machine) and finish freezing according to the manufacturer's instructions.

Freeze in an airtight container for up to 1 month.

INGREDIENTS

- 4 cups half-and-half
- 2 large eggs
- 5 large egg yolks
- 6 tablespoons granulated sugar, plus ¾ cup
- ½ cup packed light brown sugar
- ¼ teaspoon salt
- 1 tablespoon pure vanilla extract
- ¼ teaspoon pure almond extract
- 2 pounds fresh, ripe peaches, peeled, pitted, and chopped
- 1 cup heavy cream

cashew butter
ice cream sandwiches

INGREDIENTS

1   cup roasted and salted
    cashews

½   cup glutinous rice flour

¼   cup millet flour

¼   cup tapioca flour

½   cup cornstarch

¼   teaspoon baking soda

1   teaspoon guar gum

¼   teaspoon kosher salt

½   cup (1 stick) unsalted butter
    at room temperature

1   cup packed light brown
    sugar

¼   cup granulated sugar

2   large eggs

2¼ teaspoons pure vanilla
    extract

1   quart Rum Raisin Ice Cream
    (page 182)

I wanted to make some ice cream sandwiches one day, but what cookies to make? I couldn't do peanut butter, as my son, Leo, is deathly allergic to peanuts, so I decided to create a fabulous alternative: roasted cashew butter cookies. These are supremely moist and the perfect cookies for ice cream sandwiches.

MAKES 12 ICE CREAM SANDWICHES

Position an oven rack in the center of the oven. Preheat the oven to 330°F. Line two baking sheets with parchment paper or silicone baking mats.

In a blender or food processor, process the cashews until finely ground.

In a medium bowl, combine all the dry ingredients except the sugars. Stir with a whisk to blend.

In a stand mixer fitted with the paddle attachment, cream the butter, ground cashews, and the sugars on medium speed until light and fluffy. Gradually beat in the dry ingredients until blended. Beat in the eggs, one at a time, until smooth, stopping to scrape down the sides of the bowl. Beat in the vanilla.

Cover and refrigerate for 1 hour. Using a 1½-inch-diameter ice-cream scoop, spoon out little balls of dough, gently roll them between your palms, and place them 1 inch apart on the prepared pans. You should have 24 cookies. Gently press the top of each mound with a fork that has been dipped in sugar. Bake one pan at a time for 15 minutes, or until the cookies are lightly browned around the edges.

Remove from the oven and let cool for 5 minutes on the pan on a wire rack. Transfer the cookies to wire racks to cool completely.

Line a small jellyroll pan with parchment paper. Spread the bottom of a cookie with a generous scoop of ice cream and top that with another cookie, bottom-side down, pressing it to make the cookies adhere. Place on the prepared pan. Working quickly, repeat to sandwich all the cookies. Place the sandwiches in the freezer for 1 hour to set.

To store, wrap in plastic wrap and freeze for up to 1 month.

rum raisin ice cream

6 tablespoons dark rum

1 cup raisins

1 cup whole milk

1 cup heavy cream

½ cup sugar

6 large egg yolks

one 14-ounce can sweetened condensed milk

Pour the rum over the raisins in a small bowl and let stand for at least 2 hours or until the raisins have absorbed the rum.

In a small, heavy saucepan, combine the whole milk and the cream. Cook over medium-low heat until bubbles form around the edges of the pan.

Meanwhile, in a small bowl, whisk together the sugar and egg yolks until a slowly dissolving ribbon forms on the surface when the whisk is lifted.

Gradually whisk the hot milk into the egg mixture. Return to the pan and cook over medium heat, stirring constantly, until the mixture thickens enough to coat the back of a spoon. Do not boil. Whisk in the sweetened condensed milk and the raisins. Let cool, then cover and refrigerate for at least 2 hours or overnight. Freeze in an ice-cream maker, following the manufacturer's instructions.

blackberry-lemon trifles

Let's face it: As humans, we are invariably visual. We love to see beauty; to appreciate that which moves us, to see how things work, and to learn what it is we like and don't like. A visually pleasing dessert has the same effect on people as a beautiful woman entering the room. Like all truly beautiful women, this dessert is gorgeous both inside and out.

INGREDIENTS

Lemon Cake

6 tablespoons sorghum flour

6 tablespoons cornstarch

4 tablespoons tapioca flour

2 teaspoons baking powder

3 teaspoons guar gum

8 large eggs

1 cup plus 2 tablespoons sugar

1 cup (2 sticks) unsalted butter, melted

zest of 2 Meyer lemons

Vanilla Custard

2 cups whole milk

¾ cup sugar

2½ tablespoons cornstarch

2 large eggs

6 large egg yolks

2 teaspoons pure vanilla extract

Almond Chantilly Cream

3 cups heavy cream

3 tablespoons sugar

½ teaspoon pure almond extract

1½ cup sliced almonds, toasted (see page 120)

4 cups fresh blackberries

sliced almonds for garnish

MAKES 8 INDIVIDUAL TRIFLES

For the cake: Position an oven rack in the center of the oven. Preheat the oven to 350°F. Butter a jellyroll pan and line it with parchment paper. Butter the paper.

In a small bowl, combine all the dry ingredients, except the sugar, and stir with a small whisk to blend. In a stand mixer fitted with the whisk attachment, beat the eggs and sugar until doubled in volume, 2 to 3 minutes.

In three increments, gradually fold the dry ingredients into the egg mixture. Fold in the butter, then the lemon zest. Pour into the prepared pan, smooth the top, and bake for 15 to 20 minutes, or until the cake has pulled away from the sides of the pan and is set and springy when touched. Remove from the oven and let cool completely in the pan on a wire rack.

For the custard: In a small, heavy saucepan, cook the milk over medium-low heat until bubbles form around the edges of the pan. Meanwhile, in a medium bowl, combine the sugar and cornstarch and whisk until no lumps remain. Add the eggs and egg yolks and whisk until the sugar is dissolved and the mixture is fluffy.

Gradually whisk the hot milk into the egg mixture. Whisk in the vanilla. Return to the pan and cook, stirring constantly, over medium heat until thickened enough to coat the back of the spoon, 6 to 10 minutes. Remove from the heat and let cool. Cover and refrigerate for at least 2 hours or overnight.

For the cream: In a deep bowl, beat the cream until soft peaks form. Add the sugar and almond extract and beat until stiff peaks form. Fold in the almonds.

Choose 8 cylindrical glasses with a base about 2¾ inches in diameter. Choose a cookie cutter that is slightly smaller. Cut out 24 rounds from the cake and place one in the bottom of each glass. Add a layer of blackberries, then a thin layer of custard, and finally a layer of the almond cream. Repeat this process until each glass is full. Stud the final layer of almond cream with almonds for garnish.

Refrigerate for at least 30 minutes or up to 3 hours before serving.

Cover with plastic wrap and store in the refrigerator for up to 2 days.

orange-mint soufflé

While experimenting with cold soufflés, I infused cream with anything. This seemingly odd combination of flavors was nature's doing. The orange flavor is mellow and the mint is bright. Orange mint can be found at farmers' markets and garden centers during the summer months. Regular mint and ¼ teaspoon orange extract may be substituted.

MAKES ONE 8-INCH SOUFFLÉ; SERVES 8

Cut a piece of aluminum foil 28 inches long and fold it in half lengthwise so it is 6 inches wide. Wrap the aluminum collar around the top of a soufflé dish so that it extends 5 inches above the rim of the dish and fasten it with clear tape.

In a heavy, medium saucepan, combine the milk, 1 cup of the sugar, the 1 cup orange mint leaves, and orange zest. Cook over medium-low heat until bubbles form around the edges of the pan. Remove from the heat and let stand to infuse the mint and zest.

If using the gelatin sheets, place them in a shallow pan and add water to cover; let stand for 5 minutes. If using granulated gelatin, sprinkle it over the ⅓ cup water and let stand for 5 minutes.

In a stand mixer fitted with the whisk attachment, combine ½ cup of the remaining sugar and the egg yolks. Beat on high speed for 2 to 3 minutes, or until the mixture thickens enough so that a slowly dissolving ribbon forms on the surface when the beaters are lifted.

Strain the milk mixture into a large bowl. With the mixer running, ladle in the hot milk, one cup at a time. Return to the pan and cook over medium heat, stirring constantly, for about 5 minutes, or until the custard thickens enough to coat the back of a spoon. Remove from the heat.

If using the gelatin sheets, squeeze the excess water from them and whisk them into the warm custard until smooth. If using granulated gelatin, whisk the gelatin mixture into the custard until smooth. Set the bowl in a large bowl filled with ice cubes and let cool for about 15 minutes, whisking frequently.

In a stand mixer fitted with the whisk attachment, beat the cream until soft peaks form; fold into the cooled custard with a rubber spatula. In another bowl, with cleaned whisk beaters, beat the egg whites with a pinch of salt until they are frothy, then add the remaining 2 tablespoons sugar and beat until stiff, glossy peaks form. Immediately fold the meringue into the custard base until smooth. Pour the batter into the prepared dish and refrigerate for at least 4 hours or overnight.

To serve, remove the collar and present the dramatic soufflé at the table. Spoon out the portions and garnish each with a mint sprig.

INGREDIENTS

3 cups whole milk

1½ cups sugar, plus
   2 tablespoons

1 cup packed fresh orange
   mint leaves, plus sprigs
   for garnish

zest of 1 orange

7 gelatin sheets, or
   2 tablespoons plus
   1 teaspoon unflavored
   granulated gelatin

⅓ cup water for granulated
   gelatin

7 large egg yolks

1½ cups heavy cream

5 large egg whites

apricot clafoutis

During my sojourn in France, I was stunned to see how passionate the French were about their confiture (fruit preserves) making. I would see townspeople with ten-pound bags of apricots and equally large bags of sugar as they marched home to prepare their prized confections. Curious, I thought I would see what all the fuss was about and decided to buy a few apricots to taste them. My taste buds stood at attention and salivated for more of that tart sweet flesh. Then I imagined what it would be like enrobed in a custard. Here's my take on clafoutis, which is traditionally made with fresh cherries.

SERVES 6 TO 8

Position an oven rack in the center of the oven. Preheat the oven to 350°F. Generously butter a 9-by-3-inch porcelain dish and sprinkle it with cornstarch; shake and tilt to coat the dish evenly, then knock out the excess cornstarch.

Score the bottom of each apricot with an X. In a large saucepan of boiling water, blanch the apricots for 3 minutes. Using a slotted spoon, immediately transfer them to a bowl of water with ice cubes. The skins should contract and peel right off.

Halve and pit the apricots and arrange them on the bottom of the prepared dish, cut-side down. Set aside.

In a medium bowl, combine the cornstarch, tapioca flour, guar gum, and salt. Stir with a whisk to blend. In another bowl, combine the eggs and granulated sugar and whisk just until the eggs begin to froth. Whisk in the cream and half-and-half just until blended. Add the dry ingredients and whisk vigorously until smooth.

Pour the batter over the arranged apricots and bake for 40 minutes, or until the custard puffs up around the fruit and is lightly browned. Remove from the oven and let cool slightly or completely.

For the topping: In a medium bowl, whisk together the crème fraîche, mascarpone, and confectioners' sugar until smooth.

Dust the clafoutis with confectioners' sugar. Cut into wedges and serve topped with a generous dollop of the cream topping.

Serve within a few hours of baking for the best results. Refrigerate, lightly wrapped, for up to 2 days.

INGREDIENTS

8 fresh apricots

¼ cup cornstarch, plus more for sprinkling pan

¼ cup tapioca flour

2 teaspoons guar gum

⅛ teaspoon salt

3 large eggs

¾ cup granulated sugar

¾ cup heavy cream

¾ cup half-and-half

Topping

2 cups crème fraîche

⅓ cup mascarpone cheese

3 tablespoons confectioners' sugar, sifted

confectioners' sugar for dusting

CHAPTER SEVEN

dinner-party showstoppers

elderflower blancmanges

My dear friend Knoxy inspired this recipe. She asked me if I had ever had elderflower liqueur and when I said no, her eyebrows rose in surprise, and she soon brought me a bottle to experiment with in cooking. Boy, am I glad she did. With its sweet floral top note and a subtle musky base note, my taste buds went bonkers and my mind raced with culinary ideas. *Blancmange,* which literally translates from French as "white food," has been a very popular molded dessert for centuries. It is traditionally flavored with orange flower water, but elderflower gives it a whole new dimension.

SERVES 4

Lightly coat four 8-ounce decorative molds with nonstick cooking spray and set aside.

In a small, heavy saucepan, combine the milk and almond meal. Cook over medium-low heat until bubbles form around the edges of the pan. Remove from the heat and infuse for 10 minutes. Strain through a fine-mesh sieve into a bowl, pressing on the almond meal with the back of a large spoon to extract all the milk.

If using the gelatin sheets, put them in a shallow pan and add water just to cover; let stand for 5 minutes. If using granulated gelatin, sprinkle it over the 2 tablespoons plus 2 teaspoons water. Let the gelatin soften for 5 minutes. If using gelatin sheets, squeeze the excess water from them and whisk the gelatin into the hot milk mixture with the sugar until dissolved. If using granulated gelatin, whisk the gelatin mixture and sugar into the hot milk mixture until dissolved.

In a deep bowl, beat the cream until it forms soft peaks. Using a whisk, stir the cream into the warm milk mixture along with the liqueur. Pour into the prepared molds and refrigerate until set, about 2 hours.

In a small saucepan, combine the marmalade and water. Cook over low heat until melted. Spoon onto dessert plates.

To unmold the blancmanges, submerge the bottom of each mold in warm water for a few seconds and then invert the blancmange on top of the marmalade. Garnish with a few pieces of the candied lemon peel.

The blancmanges can be covered and refrigerated for up to 5 days, and the remaining lemon peel can be stored in an airtight container for up to 3 months.

INGREDIENTS

nonstick cooking spray or clarified butter (page 15)

2 cups whole milk

1½ cups almond meal

4 gelatin sheets, or 4 teaspoons unflavored granulated gelatin

2 tablespoons plus 2 teaspoons water for granulated gelatin

½ cup sugar

1½ cups heavy cream

2 tablespoons elderflower liqueur, preferably St. Germain

1 cup lemon, orange, and grapefruit marmalade, such as Dundee

¼ cup water

Candied Lemon Peel (page 194)

candied lemon peel

MAKES ABOUT ¼ CUP

2 lemons, scrubbed

⅓ cup sugar, plus more for coating

3 tablespoons water

Cut both ends from a lemon. Using a very sharp knife or a vegetable peeler, cut the yellow zest from the lemon, leaving the bitter white pith behind. Julienne the lemon peel. Repeat this process with the second lemon. In a small, heavy nonreactive saucepan, combine the ⅓ cup sugar and the water and cook over medium-high heat, stirring at first to dissolve the sugar, until the mixture begins to boil. Add the lemon zest and cook for 1 minute.

Using a slotted spoon, transfer the lemon zest to a plate. Separate the strips of lemon zest and toss in granulated sugar to coat. Spread on a baking sheet or wire rack to dry, about 1 hour.

pistachio bavarian cream charlotte

Molded desserts are exercises in architecture. Their presentations are so stunning, they are the perfect dinner-party showstopper. This one is a prime example. It's made with Bavarian cream, which is basic pastry cream set with gelatin and was created by a the famous French chef Marie-Antoine Carême, who was working in Bavaria at the time. He also invented the charlotte, by lining a mold with ladyfingers and filling it with Bavarian cream. This one is flavored with pistachios and garnished with pale green Chantilly cream.

SERVES 6

Note: For this recipe, you will need a 4-cup charlotte mold, which can be found in kitchenware shops.

For the Bavarian cream: In a heavy, medium saucepan, combine the milk, ¼ cup of the sugar, the pistachios, and almond meal. Bring just to a boil over medium heat. Remove from the heat and let stand for 1 hour. Strain through a fine-mesh sieve into a bowl, pressing on the nuts with the back of a large spoon to extract all the milk. Rinse your saucepan and set aside.

Meanwhile, in a medium bowl, whisk together the egg yolks and the remaining ½ cup sugar until a slowly dissolving ribbon forms on the surface when the whisk is lifted.

Place the gelatin sheets in a shallow bowl and cover with water to soften; let stand for 5 minutes. Or, if using granulated gelatin, sprinkle it over the ½ cup plus 2 tablespoons water to soften for 5 minutes.

Return the pistachio-infused milk to the saucepan and heat over low heat until bubbles form around the edges of the pan. Remove from the heat and gradually whisk the warm milk into the egg mixture. Return to the pan and cook over medium-low heat, stirring constantly, until the custard coats the back of a spoon. Do not boil. Remove from the heat and whisk in the almond extract.

If using gelatin sheets, squeeze out the excess water and whisk the gelatin into the custard until smooth. If using granulated gelatin, add the gelatin mixture to the custard and whisk until smooth. If your custard is very pale, add green food coloring one drop at a time. In a deep bowl, beat the heavy cream until firm peaks form; fold into the custard.

continued

INGREDIENTS

Bavarian Cream

3 cups whole milk

¾ cup sugar

1 cup ground roasted and salted pistachios (see Tip)

½ cup almond meal

8 large egg yolks

5 gelatin sheets, or 5 teaspoons unflavored granulated gelatin

½ cup plus 2 tablespoons water for the granulated gelatin

1½ teaspoons almond extract

1 cup heavy cream

1 to 5 drops green food coloring (optional)

12 Ladyfingers (page 62)

Chantilly Cream

1 cup heavy cream

1 teaspoon almond extract

1 tablespoon sugar

1 or 2 drops green food coloring

pistachio bavarian cream charlotte, continued

Strain the custard through a fine-mesh sieve into a bowl and set the bowl in a large bowl of ice cubes. Let cool, stirring frequently, until the custard is thick enough to hold its shape in a spoon. Fold in the whipped cream and remove from the ice bath.

Cut 6 to 8 ladyfingers lengthwise. Arrange these pieces to cover the bottom of the mold in the shape of a flower, with the cut-side of the ladyfingers facing up. Line the sides of the mold with the remaining lady-fingers, cut-side in.

Fill the mold with the Bavarian cream. Cut the protruding ladyfingers even with the top of the mold. Cover and refrigerate for at least 3 hours, or overnight.

For the Chantilly cream: In a stand mixer fitted with the whisk attachment, beat the cream on medium speed until it begins to form soft folds. Add the almond extract and sugar and beat on high speed until the mixture forms stiff peaks. Remove the bowl from the mixer and, using a rubber spatula, fold in the food coloring until blended.

Unmold the charlotte onto a serving plate. Put the Chantilly cream in a pastry bag fitted with a small star tip and pipe cream in the spaces between the ladyfingers. Cut into wedges to serve.

BLACKBIRD BAKING TIP

When purchasing pistachios, look for bright green ones. The paler the color, the older and longer they have been sitting around, leaving the nuts severely depleted in flavor as well as color. This lack of color will give you a very pale custard with even less flavor.

yogurt charlottes with an apple-cherry compote

I adore this recipe because you can make it a couple of days in advance, and it is visually gorgeous. The pale yogurt against the deep maroon of the compote is nothing short of enticing, and no element is overly sweet. Of all the recipes I discovered while in France, this was the one that captured my heart.

INGREDIENTS

Compote

2 pounds fresh Bing cherries, pitted

3 pears, such as Comice

2 Gala or Fuji apples, peeled, cored, and sliced

3 Golden Delicious apples, peeled, cored, and sliced

⅔ cup sugar

zest of ½ lemon

Charlottes

1 gelatin sheet, or 1 teaspoon unflavored granulated gelatin

2 teaspoons water for the granulated gelatin

⅔ cup heavy cream

⅓ cup sugar

1 cup plain whole-milk yogurt

SERVES 4

Note: For this recipe, you will need four 4-ounce charlotte molds, which can be found in kitchenware shops.

For the compote: In a large, heavy nonreactive saucepan, combine the cherries, pears, apples, sugar, and lemon zest. Gently toss to evenly coat the fruit with the sugar. Cook over low heat for 2 hours, stirring occasionally. The fruit should cook down to one-third or one-fourth of its original volume and the juices will be thickened. Remove from the heat and let cool completely in the pan. Cover and refrigerate for 24 hours.

For the charlottes: Liberally butter four 4-ounce charlotte molds. If using a gelatin sheet, place it in a shallow bowl and fill with enough water to just cover the sheet; let soften for 5 minutes. If using granulated gelatin, sprinkle it over the 2 teaspoons water to soften for 5 minutes.

In a deep bowl, beat ⅓ cup of the heavy cream just until it holds soft folds; set aside.

In a small, heavy saucepan, combine the remaining ⅓ cup heavy cream with the sugar. Cook over low heat, stirring at first to dissolve the sugar, until bubbles form around the edges of the pan. Remove from the heat. If using the gelatin sheet, squeeze out the excess water and whisk the gelatin into the hot cream mixture until smooth. If using the granulated gelatin, whisk the gelatin mixture into the hot cream until smooth.

Pour the yogurt into a small bowl and stir with a whisk until smooth. Pour the hot cream mixture into the yogurt and whisk until incorporated. Fold in the whipped cream.

Divide the yogurt mixture evenly among the prepared charlotte molds. Cover and refrigerate for at least 4 hours or up to 3 days. Dip the bottom of a charlotte mold in a bowl of hot water, then unmold the charlotte into a shallow bowl. Repeat to unmold the remaining charlottes. To serve, spoon a generous amount of the fruit compote around each charlotte.

Meringue

1½ cups sugar

2 teaspoons cornstarch

6 large egg whites

1 teaspoon distilled white vinegar

¼ cup boiling water

1½ teaspoons pure vanilla extract

Whipped Cream

2 cups heavy cream

2 tablespoons sugar

½ teaspoon pure vanilla extract

⅓ teaspoon pure almond extract

4 cups mixed fresh fruit, such as blueberries, blackberries, red currants, gooseberries, strawberries, and/or raspberries

pavlova

This favorite dessert of Australia was named after Russian ballerina Anna Pavlova by a chef who wanted to create something "as light and ethereal as the dancer herself." He achieved his goal with this meringue crust topped with whipped cream and an assortment of fresh fruit. This recipe was given to me by my ex-brother-in-law, Clayton, and it was one of the first desserts I actually enjoyed after my diagnosis.

SERVES 8

For the meringue: Position an oven rack in the center of the oven. Preheat the oven to 350°F. Line a baking sheet with parchment paper and trace a 12-inch round on the paper with a pencil.

In a medium bowl, combine the sugar and cornstarch. Stir with a whisk until smooth. In a stand mixer fitted with the whisk attachment, beat the egg whites on high speed until they begin to froth and turn opaque. Decrease mixer speed to low, and add the sugar mixture in ½-cup increments, immediately followed by the vinegar. Continue to beat on high speed for at least 2 minutes, until the whites form stiff peaks. Increase mixer speed to high and pour the boiling water into the egg whites all at once. The egg whites will swell up considerably. Beat the egg whites until the water is totally incorporated, stopping once to scrape down the sides of the bowl. Add the vanilla and continue to beat for 3 to 5 minutes, or until the egg whites form stiff, glossy peaks.

With a rubber spatula, take some of the meringue and carefully fill in the base of the traced circle. Continue to add meringue to make a thick cake.

Bake for 10 minutes, then reduce the oven temperature to 200°F and bake for 40 minutes, or until set.

Remove from the oven and let cool completely on the pan on a wire rack. Gently remove the parchment paper by rolling it out from under the meringue; take care, as the meringue will be very delicate.

For the whipped cream: In a deep bowl, beat the cream until it begins to hold its shape. Add the sugar and the vanilla and almond extract. Beat until soft peaks form.

Carefully spread the whipped cream over the top of the meringue and top with the mixed fresh fruit. Serve at once, cut into wedges.

The baked meringue can be refrigerated and lightly covered for up to 2 days.

BLACKBIRD BAKING TIP

If using sliced peaches or nectarines, toss them in a little lemon juice with 1 teaspoon of sugar to prevent them from browning.

bananas foster savarin with crème mousseline

"The discovery of a new dish does more for the human spirit than the discovery of a star."
  —Jean Anthelme Brillat-Savarin

A savarin is a yeast cake that has been soaked in a syrup infused with either rum or kirsch and is served either hot or cold, with cooked or uncooked fruit. For this recipe, I couldn't resist serving the savarin at room temperature with warm bananas Foster and mousseline cream. The savarin was named after Jean Anthelme Brillat-Savarin (1755–1826), the culinary genius who was born in Belley, a few hours south of the town where I cooked in France.

SERVES 10

Note: For this recipe, you will need a 9-inch-diameter savarin ring, which can be found in kitchenware shops.

For the savarin: Soak the golden raisins in the rum until they have absorbed all the liquid, 1 to 2 hours.

In a glass measuring cup, sprinkle the yeast over the warm milk and stir to dissolve. Set aside until foamy, about 5 minutes.

In a large bowl, combine the rest of the dry ingredients except the sugar and stir with a whisk to blend. Add the yeast mixture and eggs to the dry ingredients and stir until blended.

In a stand mixer fitted with the paddle attachment, cream together the butter and the granulated sugar until smooth.

Transfer the dough to the mixer and beat on medium-high speed until the dough pulls away from the sides of the bowl. Add the rum-soaked raisins and mix again just until the raisins are incorporated.

Coat a large bowl with nonstick cooking spray. Transfer the dough to the bowl and turn the dough to coat with oil. Cover the bowl with a damp cloth and let rise in a warm place for 1 hour, or until doubled in volume.

Position an oven rack in the center of the oven. Preheat the oven to 400°F. Coat the savarin ring with nonstick cooking spray and fill it with the dough. Smooth the top of the dough.

continued

INGREDIENTS

Savarin

¼ cup golden raisins

2 tablespoons dark rum

1 package (¼-ounce) active dry yeast

½ cup plus ⅓ cup warm whole milk (110°F)

1 cup gluten-free oat flour

½ cup chestnut flour

¾ cup glutinous rice flour

2½ teaspoons guar gum

1 teaspoon kosher salt

4 large eggs, beaten

5 tablespoons unsalted butter at room temperature

2 tablespoons granulated sugar

nonstick cooking spray

Soaking Syrup

2½ cups water

2½ cups granulated sugar

1½ teaspoons pure vanilla extract

⅔ cup dark rum

½ teaspoon ground nutmeg

Bananas Foster

3 tablespoons dark raisins

¼ cup dark rum

3 tablespoons unsalted butter

2 tablespoons light brown sugar

1 tablespoon dark brown sugar

¼ teaspoon ground cinnamon

1 tablespoon water

1 vanilla bean, split lengthwise

3 ripe bananas

Crème Mousseline (page 205)

Bake for 20 to 25 minutes, or until golden brown. Remove the savarin from the oven and unmold onto a wire rack to cool completely.

For the syrup: In a 12-inch-diameter saucepan at least 4 inches deep, combine the water and sugar. Cook, stirring, over medium heat until the sugar has dissolved, 3 to 4 minutes. Stir in the vanilla extract, rum, and nutmeg. Choose a round wire rack and tie two lengths of kitchen twine on each side long enough to overlap the side of the syrup pan by several inches. When you lift the strings, they should form a pyramid. Place the savarin on the wire rack and lower the rack into the syrup by holding the twine, making sure to let the twine overlap the outside of the pan at the end. Place a 10-inch-diameter plate on top of the savarin to keep it submerged. Let stand for 25 minutes. Remove the plate from the savarin. Lift the savarin from the soaking syrup by pulling on the ends of the kitchen twine. Transfer the wire rack and savarin to a jellyroll pan to drain for 20 minutes. Now, place the savarin ring on top of the savarin, invert the wire rack and allow the savarin to rest in its pan while you prepare the bananas Foster. Reserve the soaking syrup.

For the bananas Foster: Soak the raisins in the rum until most of the liquid is absorbed, about 2 hours.

In a large sauté pan, melt the butter over medium heat. Stir in the light and dark brown sugars and the cinnamon. Whisk to smooth, then add the water, rum-soaked raisins, and vanilla bean and cook for another minute.

Cut the bananas in half lengthwise and then each half into 3-inch-long diagonal pieces; add to the pan. Gently toss the bananas to coat evenly and sauté for 2 to 3 minutes, or until lightly golden. Remove from the heat and remove the vanilla bean.

To assemble, invert the savarin onto a serving dish and remove the ring. Drizzle a few spoonfuls of the reserved syrup over the top of the savarin. Fill the savarin ring with the warm bananas. Put the mousseline in a pastry bag fitted with a ½-inch star tip and pipe 10 rosettes on top of the savarin. Cut into wedges to serve. Spoon a piece of banana and syrup over each serving.

crème mousseline

Mousseline cream is essentially a variation of pastry cream; it has slightly more butter than pastry cream but less than buttercream, making it extremely versatile and the perfect vehicle for just about any flavor or essence. It is ideal for filling pastries and cakes.

MAKES 2 CUPS

2   tablespoons cornstarch

6   tablespoons sugar

1   cup plus 2 tablespoons whole milk

2   large eggs

1   large egg yolk

9   tablespoons unsalted butter at room temperature

1¼ teaspoon pure vanilla extract

In a small bowl, combine the cornstarch and 2 tablespoons of the sugar. Stir with a whisk until smooth. In a heavy, medium saucepan, whisk the cornstarch mixture into the milk and cook over medium heat, stirring frequently, until bubbles form around the edges of the pan. Remove from the heat.

In a medium bowl, whisk the eggs and egg yolk with the remaining ¼ cup sugar until a slowly dissolving ribbon forms on the surface when the whisk is lifted. Gradually whisk the hot milk into the egg mixture. Return to the pan and cook, stirring constantly, over medium heat until thick. Remove from the heat and stir in 3 tablespoons of the butter and the vanilla. Let cool, then cover and refrigerate for at least 30 minutes or overnight.

In a stand mixer fitted with the paddle attachment, cream the remaining 6 tablespoons butter until light and fluffy, 2 to 3 minutes. Fold the whipped butter into the chilled pastry cream until blended.

the roux brothers' faux puff pastry tart

This recipe is based on a tart that Michel and Albert Roux created for their London restaurant, Le Gavroche. (Now run by Albert's son Michel Jr., it boasts two Michelin stars.) The crust is made with pâte sucrée and choux paste, but it looks like puff pastry. As I had mastered gluten-free versions of both pâte sucrée and choux but still had not conquered puff pastry, I felt I had to include this not just for the visual effect, but also because it is as divine as it is clever.

MAKES ONE 12-INCH TART; SERVES 8 TO 10

Position an oven rack in the center of the oven. Preheat the oven to 400°F. Butter a 12-inch pastry ring and place it on a baking sheet lined with parchment paper.

On a work surface dusted with tapioca flour, roll out the pâte sucrée dough to a 12-inch round. Transfer the dough to the parchment paper and then place the pastry ring over the round. Press down the ring to cut out a round of dough. Remove the excess dough, leaving the ring in place to maintain the shape of the pastry while baking. Pierce the dough with a fork a dozen times for ventilation. Fit a pastry bag with a 1-inch plain tip and fill with the choux paste. Brush the edges of the pâte sucrée with water and then pipe a line of choux paste over it, being careful to make the choux as uniform as possible, as this will be the rim of the tart.

Bake for 20 minutes. After 15 minutes, perce the choux with the tip of a paring knife and bake until crust is golden brown, about 5 minutes more. Remove from the oven and let cool completely on a wire rack. Remove the ring.

In a small saucepan, melt the preserves over low heat. Force through a fine-mesh sieve with the back of a large spoon. Stir the strained preserves into the buttercream.

Just before serving, fill the tart with the buttercream and top with the fresh fruit. Cut into wedges and serve, garnished with mint sprigs.

Lightly cover and store in the refrigerator for up to 2 days.

INGREDIENTS

tapioca flour for dusting

1 recipe (1 disk) Pâte Sucrée dough, chilled (page 89)

1 recipe Pâte à Choux (page 161)

½ cup apricot preserves

1 recipe Buttercream (page 117)

1 cup fresh raspberries

1 cup fresh blackberries or blueberries

1 cup green grapes, sliced

mint sprigs for garnish

crepes mille-feuille

INGREDIENTS

3 cups strawberry preserves

3 tablespoons light corn syrup

8 ounces cream cheese at
room temperature

¼ cup crème fraîche

¼ teaspoon pure vanilla extract

¼ cup sifted confectioners'
sugar, plus more for dusting

24 Sweet Crepes (3 recipes;
page 153) made with Cognac

1 recipe Dark Chocolate
Custard (page 175)

8 fresh strawberries for
garnish

8 mint sprigs for garnish

Nothing says drama like layer upon layer of refinement. *Mille-feuille* literally means "a thousand leaves" and refers to the strata of puff pastry dough. I've substituted crepes in place of puff pastry, layering them with three different fillings. The beauty of this recipe is that it can be prepared up to two days in advance saving time for other dinner party preparations while making the compliments all the sweeter.

SERVES 8

Heat the strawberry preserves with the corn syrup in a saucepan and then press through a fine-mesh sieve into a bowl with the back of a large spoon.

In a stand mixer fitted with the paddle attachment, beat the cream cheese on medium-high speed until smooth. Add the crème fraîche, vanilla, and the ¼ cup confectioners' sugar, and beat just until blended.

Place a single crepe flat on a serving plate. Using an offset spatula, spread the crepe with a very thin layer of the strawberry preserves. Align another crepe over the first and spread with a very thin layer of the cream cheese mixture. Cover this with another crepe and spread with a thin layer of chocolate custard. Repeat to use the remaining crepes, with the top of the last crepe left uncovered. You should have some strawberry preserves left at this point. Set aside. Cover and refrigerate for at least 4 hours or up to 2 days.

An hour before serving, remove the mille-feuille from the refrigerator. (If the cake is too cold, the confectioners' sugar will dissolve as the cake warms.) Dust the cake with confectioners' sugar. Reheat the reserved strawberry preserves and dip the strawberries in them, coating evenly. Garnish the cake with mint sprigs and the glazed strawberries. Cut into wedges to serve.

tiramisù

¾ cup freshly brewed espresso

½ cup Calvados

3 large eggs, separated

¼ cup sugar, plus 1 teaspoon

1 teaspoon pure vanilla extract

1½ cups mascarpone cheese
   at room temperature

kosher salt

12 Ladyfingers (page 62)

1 ounce semisweet chocolate,
   grated

Here is my take on the Italian classic. I honestly thought I'd never get a chance to enjoy this dessert again, until I came up with the recipe for ladyfingers. After that, I went hog wild. The key here is to use very good, strong espresso and an equally good, smooth Calvados.

SERVES 6

Pour the espresso and Calvados into a shallow bowl and set aside. In a medium bowl, whisk together the egg yolks and the ¼ cup sugar until a slowly dissolving ribbon forms on the surface when the whisk is lifted. Whisk in the vanilla and mascarpone until satin smooth; set aside.

In a stand mixer with the whisk attachment, beat the egg whites with a pinch of salt until stiff peaks form. Add the 1 teaspoon sugar and whisk for about 1 minute more, or until the egg whites are glossy. Fold the mascarpone mixture into the egg whites and set aside.

Dip each ladyfinger in the espresso mixture, being careful to evenly coat both sides. Gently place the ladyfingers in the bottom of an 8-inch square baking dish. Cover the ladyfingers with the mascarpone mixture and smooth the top. Sprinkle with the grated chocolate. Cover and refrigerate for at least 2 hours or overnight. To serve, spoon the tiramisù into shallow bowls.

BLACKBIRD BAKING TIP

For a dramatic presentation, select 6 individual serving dishes and cut the ladyfingers to fit before soaking them. Assemble as instructed.

pear-cardamom cakes

This recipe is simple, beautiful and delicious.

MAKES 8 INDIVIDUAL CAKES

Position an oven rack in the center of the oven. Preheat the oven to 350°F. Butter a jellyroll pan and line it with parchment paper. Butter the paper.

In a large Dutch oven, combine the water, maple syrup, the ¼ cup granulated sugar, and the ¼ cup light brown sugar. Cook over medium heat, stirring occasionally, until all the sugar has melted and the syrup has reached a steady low boil, about 5 minutes. Add the pears and cook for 15 to 20 minutes, or until fork-tender. Using a slotted spoon, transfer the pears to a wire rack set on a jellyroll pan and let cool completely.

Cut the pears into ¼-inch dice and set aside. In a stand mixer fitted with the paddle attachment, combine the rest of the dry ingredients, including the ⅔ cup granulated sugar and ⅔ cup light brown sugar, and mix on low speed to blend.

With the machine running, add the butter and beat until blended. Add the eggs, one at a time, and mix until smooth. Pour in the buttermilk and the vanilla and mix on high speed for 1 minute, or until light and fluffy.

Fold in the pears and pour the batter into the prepared pan. In a small bowl, stir together the dark and golden raisins and sprinkle them evenly over the batter. Using a rubber spatula, softly press the raisins into the batter and smooth the top.

Mix the sanding sugar with the ground cardamom until there are no visible clumps. Sprinkle the cardamom sugar evenly over the batter.

Bake for 30 minutes, or until the cake is golden brown and springy to the touch.

Remove from the oven and let cool completely in the pan on a wire rack. Using a 2-inch round cookie cutter, cut out 8 rounds from the cake and place them on a clean work surface. Using a 1-inch scalloped pastry cutter, cut out 16 more cake rounds. Stir the crème fraîche until smooth.

Spread the top of one 2-inch cake round with crème fraîche and then top with a 1-inch round.

Apply another thin layer of crème fraîche to the top of this round, then top with another 1-inch cake. Repeat until all of your cakes have been assembled.

Serve each cake garnished with a dollop of crème fraîche and a few rosemary leaves.

These cakes store very well in the refrigerator for up to 3 days in an airtight container.

INGREDIENTS

- 5 cups water
- ½ cup Grade A dark amber maple syrup
- ¼ cup granulated sugar, plus ⅔ cup
- ¼ cup packed light brown sugar, plus ⅔ cup
- 4 large pears, peeled and cored
- ¾ cup sorghum flour
- ¾ cup cornstarch
- ½ cup tapioca flour
- 1 teaspoon guar gum
- ¾ teaspoon kosher salt
- 1 teaspoon baking powder
- ¾ cup (1½ sticks) plus 2 tablespoons unsalted cultured butter at room temperature, diced
- 4 large eggs
- ½ cup organic buttermilk
- 1 tablespoon pure vanilla extract
- 2 cups dark raisins
- 1 cup golden raisins
- ¼ cup sanding sugar
- ½ teaspoon ground cardamom
- crème fraîche for serving
- rosemary sprigs for garnish

resources

ARROWHEAD MILLS
1.800.434.4246
www.arrowheadmills.com
Organic millet flour, glutinous rice flour.

AUSTIN NUTS
1.877.329.6887
Roasted cashews, almonds, and Texas pecans.

B & G FOODS
1.888.887.3268
www.bgfoods.com
Molasses.

BOB'S RED MILL NATURAL FOODS
www.bobsredmill.com
All-purpose gluten-free flour mix, sorghum flour, tapioca flour, white rice flour.

DAILY JUICE
512.480.9501
www.dailyjuice.com
Fresh young-coconut juice.

GUITTARD CHOCOLATE COMPANY
650.697.4424
www.guittard.com
Superb milk and dark chocolate chips.

KALUSTYAN'S
212.685.3451
www.kalustyans.com
Medjool dates, candied cherries, tapioca flour, glutinous rice flour, chestnut flour.

NAVITAS NATURALS
1.888.645.4292
www.navitasnaturals.com
Chia seeds.

NOW FOODS
1.888.669.3663
www.nowfoods.com
Guar gum.

PENZEYS SPICES
1.800.741.7787
www.penzeys.com
Vietnamese cinnamon, Mexican vanilla extract, pure almond extract.

SCHARFFEN BERGER CHOCOLATE
1.866.608.6944
www.scharffenberger.com
Unsweetened and bittersweet chocolate.

ST. GERMAIN LIQUEUR
www.stgermain.fr
Elderflower liqueur.

SUR LA TABLE
512.833.9605
www.surlatable.com
Savarin rings, pastry rings, charlotte molds, ramekins, tart and tartlet pans.

WHOLE FOODS MARKETS
www.wholefoodsmarket.com
Gluten-free products.

WILLIAMS-SONOMA, INC.
1.877.812.6235
www.williams-sonoma.com
Sanding sugar, gelatin sheets, bakeware.

table of equivalents

The exact equivalents in the following tables have been rounded for convenience.

LIQUID/DRY MEASUREMENTS

U.S.	METRIC
¼ teaspoon	1.25 milliliters
½ teaspoon	2.5 milliliters
1 teaspoon	5 milliliters
1 tablespoon (3 teaspoons)	15 milliliters
1 fluid ounce (2 tablespoons)	30 milliliters
¼ cup	60 milliliters
⅓ cup	80 milliliters
½ cup	120 milliliters
1 cup	240 milliliters
1 pint (2 cups)	480 milliliters
1 quart (4 cups/32 ounces)	960 milliliters
1 gallon (4 quarts)	3.84 liters
1 ounce (by weight)	28 grams
1 pound	448 grams
2.2 pounds	1 kilogram

LENGTHS

U.S.	METRIC
⅛ inch	3 millimeters
¼ inch	6 millimeters
½ inch	12 millimeters
1 inch	2.5 centimeters

OVEN TEMPERATURE

FAHRENHEIT	CELSIUS	GAS
250	120	½
275	140	1
300	150	2
325	160	3
350	180	4
375	190	5
400	200	6
425	220	7
450	230	8
475	240	9
500	260	10